HOW TO TALK TO ANGELS

© Roxanne Lavallee Photography

About the Author

Lucinda M. Gabriel, a civil engineer by profession, decided after many years to follow her soul's calling to write, teach, and inspire. Now an author, speaker, and respected medium, she is also a certified Reiki Master. She studied Angel Therapy with bestselling author Doreen Virtue as well as advanced mediumship with renowned medium Lisa Williams.

HOW TO TALK TO ANGELS

A PRACTICAL GUIDE TO ASKING FOR GUIDANCE, COMFORT & STRENGTH

LUCINDA GABRIEL

Llewellyn Publications
Woodbury, Minnesota

FIRST EDITION
First Printing, 2017

Cover design: Ellen Lawson

Llewellyn Publications is a registered trademark of Llewellyn Worldwide Ltd.

Library of Congress Cataloging-in-Publication Data
Names: Gabriel, Lucinda, author.
Title: How to talk to angels : a practical guide to asking for guidance, comfort, and strength / by Lucinda Gabriel.
Description: FIRST EDITION. | Woodbury : Llewellyn Worldwide, Ltd, 2017.
Identifiers: LCCN 2016047266 (print) | LCCN 2017001437 (ebook) | ISBN 9780738750484 | ISBN 9780738751504 (ebook)
Subjects: LCSH: Angels.
Classification: LCC BL477 .G24 2017 (print) | LCC BL477 (ebook) | DDC 202/.15—dc23
LC record available at https://lccn.loc.gov/2016047266

Llewellyn Publications
A Division of Llewellyn Worldwide Ltd.
2143 Wooddale Drive
Woodbury, MN 55125.2989
www.llewellyn.com

Printed in the United States of America

Other Books by Lucinda Gabriel

Nos Anges au Ciel
(Les Éditions Le Dauphin Blanc, 2016)

L'Amour Divin et les Anges
(Les Éditions Le Dauphin Blanc, 2015)

Comment Parler aux Anges!
(Les Éditions Le Dauphin Blanc, 2013)

Dedication

To all of you who, like me, are seeking a sense of meaning in your life, I dedicate this book with all my heart. May it comfort you, connect you with your loving angels and guides, and carry you through difficult times. Know that you are never alone. You are immensely loved by God and the angels and are destined to have a magnificent life beyond anything you can even imagine!

Contents

Exercises

Acknowledgments

First and foremost I would like to thank my loving angels for urging me to write this book. Thank you for guiding me toward my French publisher, Les Éditions Le Dauphin Blanc, and for making this book such a big success in French. Thank you for guiding me toward Llewellyn Worldwide, who graciously offered to publish this book in English. I am so grateful to you, my loving angels, for your wonderful and clear guidance in my life. It is my greatest desire to share your presence and love with the world.

Thank you to everyone at Llewellyn Worldwide and particularly Amy Glaser, acquisitions editor of paranormal subjects, for believing in my book from day one. I am truly grateful to all of the team at Llewellyn for their hard work and dedication to publishing excellent metaphysical books and resources.

Thank you to my mom, Elaine Letemplier, for helping me with the translation. Thank you for believing in me and for your love and support in all that I do.

A special thank you to my cousin Paulette Losier for taking the time to read and correct the English version of this book. I greatly appreciate you taking the time to help me get my message out to the world.

A big thank you to my family, my mom Elaine, my brother Kirby, my sister Karen and her husband, Roylie, as well as my niece and nephew Mandy and Steve, for all your love and support. Thank you for encouraging me to be myself and to follow my dreams. Thank you for believing in me and in all I do. I am so blessed to have such a wonderful and loving family.

Thank you to all my clients, readers, and followers. Thank you for giving my life a sense of purpose and for your confidence in me and in my work. I honor each and every one of you for believing in and listening to your angels and for having the courage to follow their guidance to manifest the wonderful life you deserve.

Namasté,

Lucinda M. Gabriel

Preface

From the first lines of the introduction, this passionate book captivated me and kept my interest from page to page, up to the last words.

In a simple style, Lucinda takes us by the hand and guides us through the world of angels that is really our world seen through a different perspective. She answers questions that many people ask, relates numerous personal experiences, and invites us to observe the signs in our lives, to open ourselves up, to discover that we are more exceptional and more aware than what we believe.

This book is a bedside book. To read it once is not enough! It motivates us to practice because it reveals the *how*: how to talk to angels, how to let ourselves be guided by our intuition, how to manifest what we wish, how to heal, how to see more clearly—in short, how to LIVE in capital letters!

—Lisette Simard, author and speaker,
life coach (PLN), and eternal student of life

INTRODUCTION

Your angels and guides want to present themselves to you. They want to assist you on this journey we call life. They want you to be happy and healthy, to experience love and abundance, and ultimately to live the life of your dreams.

This practical guide will teach you how angels talk to you. It will help you develop your intuition and your "clairs" to better receive their messages. It will also help you connect with your angels and guides so that you may begin your very own conversation with them and start manifesting the magnificent life that you are destined to live.

The angels tell me that we are meant to live a magnificent and gratifying life. The simple fact of recognizing the existence of angels embellishes our life. If we invite them into our everyday lives to accompany us on our path, if we learn how to talk to them, we can create a life greater than anything we could ever imagine, a divinely inspired life! This is what I wish to share with you in this book.

Back in 2003, I was working at a government job in Ontario. I had a beautiful apartment, a new car, and many nice things, but I was very unhappy. I felt like something really important was missing from my life. One weekend I cried out to God[1] in one of those "dark night of the soul" moments and said to him/her/it that if life was only about

---

1. I will use the word *God* for ease of writing, but it can be replaced with Spirit, Creator, Universe, or whatever word you feel most comfortable with.

working to buy things and have things, I was not interested in staying. I needed my life to have more meaning. I needed to feel useful, like I was making a difference. My soul was unhappy, my body was sick, and I was exhausted. I felt like I needed a better reason to live. I wanted to matter.

The following Monday, I met my neighbor Dorinda, who just happened to be a Reiki Master and whose name means "gift from God." Being that I was suffering greatly from ulcerative colitis at the time, she offered me a Reiki energy treatment. Meeting Dorinda and learning about Reiki was the beginning of a whole new life for me, a new spiritual life. Through her, I met a lovely group of Metis ladies and was invited to join their circle. We did monthly moon ceremonies and talking circles. This new spiritual life filled the hole that I had inside.

Next, I decided to take Reiki classes to help me heal my body, and I noticed that with every class my psychic senses started to develop. Then, through a series of events, I felt guided to take Doreen Virtue's Angel Therapy class in 2004. Dr. Virtue is the author of the bestselling books *Healing with the Angels*, *Angel Therapy*, and *The Lightworker's Way* as well as numerous angel oracle card decks.

One day, my friend Claudette arrived home from a trip to North Bay, Ontario, with a deck of cards titled *Messages from Your Angels*. It was the most beautiful deck of cards I had ever seen. The images were absolutely extraordinary.

When I shuffled the pack, one card fell out onto the table. It was "Archangel Raphael" and it said that I was a healer like him. Having just completed my first level of Reiki that same day, I was very impressed with the accuracy of the cards, so much so that I went straight to the bookstore to purchase them.

A few days later, I drove to Gatineau, Quebec, to visit my friend Odette. I was excited to show her my new deck of cards, but before

I got the chance she told me that she had just met a woman, Jennifer Clark, who talks to angels. Curious, I visited her website. When I read through her site, something spoke to the deepest part of my soul and I thought that it was the most wonderful thing someone could ever do with their life. I said to myself, "Ah! How lucky she is to have such a wonderful career!"

Going through her website, I noticed that Clark had studied with a lady named Doreen Virtue. The name sounded familiar. I went through my library to see if I had one of her books. I didn't find any. Then I noticed the oracle cards on my table that I had recently purchased and there it was—Doreen Virtue's name. What a coincidence!

I visited Doreen Virtue's website and came across her Angel Therapy class information. Once again, my heart skipped a beat and something about the whole thing spoke to me. But my ego kicked in and said, "That course is for gifted people and you don't have a gift!" So I closed down my computer and gave up on the idea that I might be "special." The course was not for me.

Over the next three days, the idea of this course kept coming back to me. It haunted me. So by Wednesday morning I looked up toward the sky and said to God, "I think you want me to take this course. So if you do, then show me the money!"

That same day, I went to work and noticed that I had an extra $150 on my pay stub. My colleagues explained that it was because we had finished paying into one of the funds and that we would receive this amount every two weeks up until Christmas. This amounted to $1,200. The course cost $1,500. So I made a mental note that I just needed another $300.

When I arrived home at the end of the day, I received a letter from my auto insurance company. The cost for insurance in Ontario is extremely high. I was so distraught by the amount that I picked up the phone and called another company. I saved $300. So I looked up to the sky once more and said to God, "I think you really, really want me to take this course. Well, I'm going to need a plane ticket."

The following Monday, I arrived home from work, and in my mailbox I found a letter from Aeroplan, Air Canada's rewards program. It said that because of the inconveniences that I had experienced during my last vacation due to the big electrical shortage that had struck Ontario, Quebec, and northern parts of the United States, I had been awarded triple reward points. This brought my points up to 42,000. I needed 40,000 to go to Hawaii.

With all these signs, I had to accept "the call."

During the course in Hawaii, I learned that angels and guides accompany each and every one of us. And since my return, I have felt guided to present at conferences and give private readings. I connect people with their guides and angels and bring them guidance regarding their path in life. I also have the privilege to connect people with their deceased loved ones and bring them healing and loving messages.

The angels wanted me to write this book for you so that you, too, can benefit from their loving presence and divine guidance. They want you to know that you are not alone and they are but a whisper away. So invite them into your life, ask them for help with anything, and see how magically your life transforms!

1

DIVINE GUIDANCE

"The eyes of Angels are such
that they can see the bottom of the heart."
—*Theodore Roszak*

We have all received signs from time to time, guiding us along our path. But we tend to explain or rationalize the ideas, inspirations, and coincidences that present themselves to us on a daily basis. But everything happens for a reason. Every thing, every person, and every song that we hear is a sign from the angels guiding us on our path. To recognize the messages, we must listen and pay attention to the signs we receive and find their meaning in our lives.

How often have you heard a song on the radio guiding you to "break away" from a job or a bad relationship and you haven't listened? Have you ever overheard a conversation and felt like the message was for you but you chose to discount it because the people conversing weren't speaking directly to you? How many times have you had the same recurring dream that you are "trapped" and then dismissed it?

I have lived these experiences. I heard the Kelly Clarkson song "Breakaway," which was guiding me to leave my well-paying government job, and I also had a recurring dream that I was trapped when

I felt trapped in an unhealthy relationship. So I understand how difficult it can be to heed the guidance. Receiving the message is sometimes the easiest part. Listening to the advice and following through on it is another story, but the angels assure us that if we do, they will meet us every step of the way. We just need to trust them, and we can build this trust over time.

Start by taking small, easier steps, like when you feel guided to go into a certain store, talk to a certain person, or start a small project. You will discover the reasons why you were guided to take a certain action. This will build your faith, and when you feel guided to take a bigger step, such as leaving a job or a bad relationship, you will feel more confident that things will work out because you will be able to look back on all the other occasions when you followed the guidance and things fell into place.

I remember back in 2002, I felt guided to leave my boyfriend at the time. I started to look for an apartment and could not find anything suitable. Only after I got up the courage to tell him how I really felt did everything fall into place. Only then did the beautiful apartment I was meant to find become available that same day. That was a leap of faith. Sometimes we want everything to be perfectly in place before we follow the guidance, but we must take it one step at a time, trusting that the next step will appear once we heed the guidance. Our angels will not let us down.

The angels tell me there are no coincidences. Signs are all around us. Our life, the people in it, and our environment are a reflection of ourselves, of our being, of our soul. Everything is speaking to us.

Let your imagination run wild and observe everything around you: the symbols and the shapes of the rocks, the marks on the wood, the images in the sky, and even the pictures hanging in your hotel room.

Also pay attention to your intuition as it guides you to seize an opportunity to travel or to offer a gift, a smile, or a compliment to someone else. The angels are there not only to serve us but also to help us serve others. We have all, at some point, felt compelled to serve another, but we resisted, telling ourselves that we were afraid to "bother" others. Stop and remind yourself that your life is not only about you and your well-being. It must also be about service to others. So if you feel compelled to give to others, follow your heart and know that you are guided by your angels to be an angel for someone else.

Even so-called negative experiences and challenges, such as separation, divorce, or a dismissal, can bring us closer to our path. Illness and delays sometimes give us the break we need to realign ourselves in the right direction.

A friend of mine was in an unhealthy relationship. She was planning her move, setting things up so she could bravely move forward when one day she arrived home to find all of her belongings on the doorstep. Her boyfriend had listened in on a conversation she'd had with a girlfriend about how she was planning on leaving him. He decided to take matters into his own hands and help her move by packing all her stuff and putting it outside. She was taken aback, but it was the nudge she needed. We laughed about it afterward. "Think of how lucky you are that you didn't even need to pack!" I told her.

Life is all about perception. We can look at any situation and see the positive or the negative. Choose to see the bright side of every situation. Ask yourself, "How is this positively affecting my life?" "What good can come of this?" "What have I learned from this situation?" There is always a good reason for everything, and life is always moving us toward our destiny. If we keep a positive attitude about any situation, we can transform it into something wonderful.

Even accidents or illnesses such as cancer, burnout, or depression can be a catalyst for change. We need to ask ourselves, "What is this trying to tell me?" Often these situations are trying to get our attention, showing us how we need to love ourselves more by putting our dreams and ourselves first.

I started to write this book at the end of 2012 while I was on sick leave for "occupational burnout." At first I was in fear; I was afraid I would never come out of it. I felt like I was just going deeper and deeper and becoming more and more depressed. I was mentally and physically exhausted and afraid my coworkers and my boss would judge me. I began to speak more frequently with my angels and ask for their guidance. I prayed to them for help. Then one day, I felt they wanted me to finally start writing a book in French. I was resisting writing in French because I was unsure if I was capable. But one night at 11:00 pm, the feeling was so strong that I just started. I actually began writing in English, and after a few pages I felt nudged to try it in French, and it just started to flow. I felt guilty for writing a book while on sick leave, but my psychologist encouraged me to do things that nourished my soul. She said that it would help me find joy in my life again. And so I did—and it did.

The time I was off work resting and recuperating helped me to see that my job no longer gave me the satisfaction it once had and that I was resisting changing my life and embracing the new life God and the angels desired for me. I had felt the urge to make a change in 2009 but resisted out of fear. I had a hundred people on my waiting list for readings but was afraid I would not survive financially. When we resist the call to change, we become exhausted, depressed, and ill. But if we continue to resist, the angels will simply change our life for us. Resisting change is like trying to paddle upstream, which is why we end up feeling burned-out and exhausted. It takes so much energy to resist. It is much easier to go with the flow and allow life to guide us downstream. We just need to get past the fear.

Challenges are really opportunities. When you find yourself before a closed door, such as pointless interviews or relationships devoid of love and respect, see these challenges as opportunities to get back on the right track. Often your soul's path is different from your ego's. Invite your angels to help you realign your course, to open your heart and your eyes to options that you would not even have imagined otherwise.

Often, after experiencing an occupational burnout or dismissal, people realize they no longer wish to do the same kind of work. For me, it was the burnout that helped me realize that what I had to give to my job was done and it was time to answer the call of my soul to share with you my knowledge of and experience with the angels.

Each time I lived through a major change in my life, the signs were always there to guide me back onto my path. I just had to summon the strength and courage to follow it. Like I said, I know this is easier said than done. I have done my share of crying while moving forward. It seems the older we get, the more difficult it is and the more fear we have. But we have to push through the fear and have faith that we are never alone.

Just the other day, I found a letter I had written to myself after I left my last boyfriend. It said, "I've always been more afraid of getting stuck in yesterday than I am of tomorrow." Tomorrow is always full of possibilities. We know what we lived through yesterday: fear, doubt, sadness, hopelessness. Tomorrow really can't be any worse if we take a chance. We need to build our faith and remember that God and the angels have always taken care of us in the past and they will do so again. We are immensely loved beyond anything we can imagine. We must hang on to that in times of change. We must remember that we are not alone and that everything will work out for our highest and greatest good. Find the lessons and move on, and move quickly. We all make bad choices at some point. As soon as you realize it, admit it and choose again.

In the next chapter, we will look at the different types of angels and guides that exist and how they can help us in our lives, but first I will answer your most frequently asked questions about angels.

Does everyone have angels and guides?

Yes, each person has at least one angel and one guide beside them, as well as archangels and ascended masters. The next chapter will give more details about them.

Why are they present?

They are all there basically for the same reason: to help guide you in this life to accomplish your life's purpose. The angels bring you the resources you need, while your guide steers you in the right direction.

How can they help us?

They can help you by guiding you in the right direction and by encouraging you not to limit yourself, to believe in your dreams and help you realize them.

Do we bother them?

You never disturb angels, guides, archangels, or masters, but if you call upon your loved ones too much, it can slow down their process into the spiritual realm. All souls go through a healing process in the spiritual realm that takes time. The length of time it takes depends on the soul and the healing it needs to do.

If we don't believe in them, are they still there?

Yes, they are with you whether you believe in them or not. They patiently wait for you to acknowledge them so they may help you. The angels cannot intervene in your life without your permission. God has given you free will, and the angels cannot go against it, unless you ask.

Can we talk to them? And if yes, how?

Yes, you can talk to them like a friend. Your angel can be your greatest confidant. Do not hesitate to share with her your deepest desires. Actually it is by talking to your angel that you will deeply feel in your heart what you truly desire, and it is your emotions that will communicate to them your most cherished dreams. So go ahead and dream! Imagine in great detail the life you desire, and begin to feel the joy, abundance, and gratitude for the imminent fulfillment of your wildest dreams.

Can they help us with love, abundance, career, and so on?

Absolutely! Angels are there mainly to help you live happily and accomplish your life's purpose. Above all, they want you to be happy and they want your earthly experience to be all that you desire it to be and more.

How can we really know they are there?

Ask your angels for a sign and pay attention to what happens. Your ego will want to rationalize the signs, but sometimes they will be so unexplainable that you will have no choice but to believe.

During my trip to Hawaii, my first flight was from Ottawa to Chicago, where I had to change planes. The aircraft was flying just above the clouds. At one point I looked out of the window and clearly saw the face of Abraham Lincoln in the clouds. The face was very big and was looking up toward the sky. I could hardly believe my eyes! Seeing images in the clouds was not new to me, but to see the face of the former president of the United States was weird even for me. I had no camera, so I could not take a picture, but I did think it was strange to see his face in particular. When we landed in Chicago, I walked toward the door of my next flight and, turning the corner, found myself face to face with a huge statue of Abraham Lincoln. Was this a coincidence or a sign from the angels?

I often wondered why I saw the face of Abraham Lincoln. I knew it was a sign from the angels and there are no coincidences. If we see something so incredible, there has to be a reason for it. I believe I received my answer many years later when I read the book *Ghosts Among Us* by James Van Praagh. James had had a visitation from Abraham Lincoln one evening. President Lincoln told him, "We are here to assist you in your mission.… We are working with you to open the hearts and minds of everyone you touch and to bring a new awareness to many."[2] I believe this message was meant for me too. When you read a book and something speaks to you, know that the message is for you. The angels go to great lengths to bring you messages, so please don't discount them. No sign is wasted.

Is it important to know the name of our angel and address them in a certain way?

That depends on you. Personally I don't think it's important. I don't like to get stuck in formalities. So I don't stop to wonder what angel could better serve me for such and such a reason. I ask, I believe, I receive, and I am grateful. I do not believe the angels, archangels, or ascended masters would be offended if you did not call them by their

---

2. James Van Praagh, *Ghosts Among Us* (New York: HarperOne, 2008), 85.

correct name. Unlike us, they have no ego. What matters most is to believe in them, to have absolute faith in their presence in your life and in their desire to accompany you, and to always be grateful.

Might we call on "bad" spirits?

I believe that if you focus on light and love, that is what you will attract. That being said, if you are afraid or are curious about the "dark side," then that is what you will attract. It is all in the intention.

God, angels, archangels, and ascended masters only want what is best for you, so stay centered in your heart and focused on love and trust them.

I personally work only with the light. I ask Archangel Michael to protect me at all times, and I always set the intention to receive messages from pure light only.

2
ANGELIC AND SPIRITUAL REALMS

"All mortals have one: this protective angel,
this invisible friend that watches over his heart."
—*Alphonse de Lamartine*

There exist two distinct realms: the angelic realm and the spiritual realm. The main difference between the two is that those from the angelic realm have never lived on earth.

The Angelic Realm

The angelic realm comprises angels, archangels, fairies, and animal spirits as well as guardian angels.

During my private consultations, I've noticed that everyone has angels and archangels around them. Angels may adopt different forms according to a person's belief system, culture, or religion. For example, people of Irish descent often have fairies instead of angels, and Native Americans are often surrounded by animal spirits.

The main archangels that I notice around people are as follows.

Archangel Michael

Archangel Michael is known to be the protector. He is always with people who have suffered abuse or have a protector role. He brings you strength, courage, and protection. He helps you with your career and your life's purpose. He is also very gifted in mechanical things. If you are nervous or anxious, ask Archangel Michael to bring you inner peace and calm. Ask him to come to you in your dreams and help you let go of your fears that are preventing you from moving forward and being all that you are meant to be.

A few years back, I was on a business trip while I was working for the government. When I arrived at the hotel, they gave me the key to my room, which was located directly across from the breakfast area and near the entrance. At that moment I had a strange sensation come over me but dismissed it. I felt that this area must have been where the bar used to be in the hotel years earlier. There weren't any other rooms available in the hotel because of new construction in the area. We actually had to book our hotel room weeks in advance.

After dinner, I settled in my room and called home. Then I turned off the light and lay back on the pillow and closed my eyes. Right then I sensed a spirit enter the room. I knew it was a male energy. With my eyes closed, I could see him come through the door, walk by the edge of the bed, and come right up next to me in record speed. My heart started to race so fast that I immediately called out "Michael!" in my head, and I saw the spirit turn around and leave at once. The energy wasn't necessarily a "bad" spirit, but I was just taken by surprise by his presence in my dark hotel room. Archangel Michael is very quick to respond in these types of situations.

Each time I leave my house, I call on Archangel Michael to protect my car, my home, the people I meet on my route, and myself.

When you call on Archangel Michael (or any other angel), I recommend that you always thank them in advance when you ask them for a favor, unless you are in an emergency situation like I was in the hotel room. For example, you could say, "Thank you, Archangel Michael, for courage." Because if you say, "Archangel Michael, give me courage," he will bring you situations to help you develop courage. But if you thank him in advance, it is like saying to him that you already have it, so the universe then reacts like you have it.

The perfect example of this is when mothers are struggling to keep it together with their children and they cry out, "Angels, give me patience today!" What happens? The angels give them more opportunities to develop patience. The children get more agitated and excited and the mothers get more exasperated. Note the difference between the two phrases "Angels, give me patience!" and "Thank you, my darling angels, for the patience." Don't you feel more patient already when you thank the angels in advance? Can you feel the different energy in those two sentences? Always be grateful in advance, because it is affirming that you already have what you need.

Archangel Raphael

Archangel Raphael is the healing angel. He is often with people who work in health care, such as doctors, nurses, and different types of energy workers. He can help you heal your physical body as well as your relationships. If you have a physical problem or an illness, imagine that Archangel Raphael is enveloping that part of your body with his beautiful emerald green light and thank him for the healing. He also helps you with your own healing process by guiding you through your intuition and by giving you signs to live a healthier lifestyle.

To heal your personal or professional relationships, say, "Archangel Raphael, thank you for helping me resolve this conflict. Thank you for helping me see this situation with love and for resolving it for the highest and greatest good of all."

Archangel Raphael also helps with money issues. He can help you pay your debts and attract abundance.

Archangel Gabriel

Archangel Gabriel is the angel of communication. He is known as the "messenger of God." He can help you with your writing if you are working on a book or thesis, and he can also help you develop your communication skills. If you are a teacher, counselor, actor, artist, or writer, Archangel Gabriel can help you develop your abilities and fine-tune your craft.

When I sense Archangel Gabriel near a person, this tells me that they have an important role to play in communications. And if they are not already working in that field, they should be. They may be a journalist, an artist, or an author. They are called to work in the arts and communication fields.

You can call on Archangel Gabriel to assist you with all forms of communication, such as in your work and in your love life as well as with your family. If you have difficulty speaking up and being assertive, he can help you find the right words to help you stand your ground and feel heard.

Sometimes Archangel Gabriel comes to you to announce good news, such as the birth of a child or a new project. He also brings hope and direction. If you need help with this, ask Archangel Gabriel for his loving guidance.

Archangel Uriel

Archangel Uriel is the light bringer. He sheds light on situations. If you need to be enlightened about any situation or your life's purpose, ask him for help. He can help you with your concentration during an exam or bring you a feeling of peace and well-being. He also inspires creative and ingenious ideas to resolve intellectual problems. He will bring you new insights into any problem you have and help you resolve any enigmas.

In the appendix you will find a list of the other archangels that you can call upon for assistance.

The Spiritual Realm

Members of the spiritual realm differ from those of the angelic realm because of their earthly experience. The spiritual realm comprises ascended masters such as Jesus, Buddha, Mother Mary, Saint Theresa, Mahomet, Quan Yin, and all other saints and prophets who lived on earth, as well as our spirit guides and deceased loved ones.

Ascended Masters

From my experience, every person has a least one or two ascended masters helping them accomplish their life's purpose. Knowing which master is with you gives an indication of your life's work.

Jesus

I often see Jesus with teachers and counselors because their role is much like his: to guide souls on the right path. Jesus Christ, or Jesus of Nazareth, is known as the Savior or Messiah come to save the world, as prophesied in the Old Testament of the Christian religion. His teachings were about love and forgiveness. He was a healer and performed miracles. He was closest to those who were most in need of forgiveness, faith, and guidance.

Mother Mary

Mother Mary is often with people who are mothers to everyone, such as the mother who cares for all the children in the neighborhood, the mother whom all the children adore. The children feel understood by her and she has a very special bond with them, particularly the "indigo" and "crystal" children.

Mother Mary is known as Jesus's mother in Christianity. She is also what most Christians believe to be the Blessed Virgin Mary. She is considered to be the mother of all children. You can call on Mary to help you with any issue related to children, including fertility, adoption, and discipline.

Mother Mary helps everyone who calls on her. During a recent visit to Quebec City, I met my uncle's new wife. She is a beautiful person who is a very strong believer. She was telling me that she prays to Saint Rita and that all her prayers are answered. So I decided to pray to Mother Mary, because in my native village of Lourdes-de-Blanc-Sablon, Quebec, there is a statue of the Virgin Mary on a cape overlooking the village. All the residents pray to her and believe in her power.

I started a novena while I was in Quebec City and continued upon my return home. On the fifth day, my friend Linda came to visit. She arrived with a big gift bag. We had been trying to get together for over a month, but our schedules were just off. I opened the bag and was astounded to see that it held a statue of the sacred heart of Mary. What a wonderful gift! The timing could not have been more perfect! Since then, the statue has held a special place in my office.

Saint Theresa

Saint Theresa of Lisieux is a saint who lived in France in the late nineteenth century. She is known to have had great healing powers. She is most often with people who care for others, such as caregivers for elderly people and politicians who care for their communities. She is also near people who pray to her and with women named Theresa or Therese. If you see or smell roses, you will know that Saint Theresa is with you.

Many more ascended masters and saints exist. If you are meant to discover them, they will surely find a way to make themselves known to you. You can go to a spiritual bookstore and browse autobiographies and books on certain masters and particular saints. You can even find bookmarks with special prayers to them. Notice if you feel attracted to a specific one. Allow yourself to be guided to the master or saint who can help you with any situation you are facing.

Spirit Guides

All of us have a least one spirit guide. A spirit guide is a soul that has already lived on earth and has lived similar challenges to our own. They are with us in this life to guide us. They help us make good decisions. They encourage us and bring us strength and courage when needed.

Half of our qualities resemble our angel's qualities, and these are mostly our feminine ones. This is the part of us that is gentle, generous, calm, and, in the case of fairies, playful. The other half of our qualities are similar to those of our guide, and tend to be more masculine. Attributes such as strength, confidence, self-esteem, resilience, and courage make up some of these.

Guides can be ancient soldiers, warriors, wise men, medicine men, scientists, priestesses, and so on. Generally they are souls that have lived many lives and have acquired the wisdom and experience to help us.

Sometimes these guides are someone quite famous. For example, I have often seen Florence Nightingale with nurses. Florence Nightingale is known as the founder of modern-day nursing. She had a strong sense of being called by God to serve others. Against her family's wishes, she studied nursing and devoted her life to helping others.

I once met an Afro-Canadian woman who was accompanied by Martin Luther King Jr., who was best known for his role in the Civil Rights movement. At the end of the consultation, I discovered that it was actually Martin Luther King Jr. Day. This lady's life purpose was important. She was destined to bring about positive changes that would help the cause of African women all over the world, and this would be done in a very public way in the years to come. At the end of the consultation, the young woman confided to me that I was not the first to tell her she was going to be significant in the African movement, but I was the first to see Martin Luther King Jr. beside her.

Deceased Loved Ones

Deceased loved ones are often beside people when there is something incomplete, like when a person needs to forgive someone or needs to be forgiven. By holding a grudge, you may be holding a deceased loved one from going further into the spiritual realm. I often meet souls, whether through my consultations or simple encounters, that are attached to the earth plane because they didn't have any spiritual beliefs or didn't believe in the afterlife. They are surprised to find that their "consciousness" continues to exist, and they seek help and guidance.

When a person dies suddenly by accident, they may be confused or refuse to believe they are dead, so they remain attached to the place where the accident occurred. Often people who commit suicide do not believe they deserve to go to heaven and they get "stuck" where they committed the act. Like in the television series *Ghost Whisperer*, a large part of my private consultation work consists of helping these souls cross over into the light. We can all pray to the angels and ask them to help our loved ones cross over, and we can also talk to our loved ones and help them believe in the afterlife and their worthiness.

Recently, during a visit to Quebec City, I had lunch with a former colleague. When we arrived at the restaurant, we ordered lunch and suddenly I felt a presence around my friend. I am very clairsentient, so I feel a spirit presence rather than see them. I asked my friend, "Who recently died that you knew?" She was surprised. She questioned why I hadn't asked her about this the last time we had seen each other a month earlier. I explained that I hadn't asked her then because I hadn't felt anyone present. But on this day, there certainly was a spirit standing next to her.

"Well, my godmother passed away last summer," she said.

"No, it's not your godmother."

"Well, now you are scaring me, Lucinda!" she said. "I just received news that a mutual friend of ours has died."

Now I was surprised. I said, "Someone I know? That we both know?"

"Yes, it's George! The police just called the office. They are looking for his parents to inform them. He was on vacation in another country and something tragic happened outside of a bar."

Then I felt George's presence even stronger. I felt that he was in shock. My friend was very uncomfortable with my gift, so I told George to stay calm and that I would talk to him a little later.

I talked to George throughout the entire week, the time it took for his body to be returned to our country. Each time I spoke to him, I felt him become calmer. We reminisced about the great times we'd had with the office crew. He found it difficult to accept that he had died so young. I explained to him that it was simply his karma, nothing more. He seemed to accept this explanation. I sensed that he was more at peace and was looking forward to attending his funeral service.

A year and a half later, I was moving to the province of New Brunswick from Quebec City and had one last client to see before the move. A lovely dark-haired lady arrived at my door. After she

sat down, I told her she was very lucky to see me since I was moving away but that I felt this reading was very important. I started the
reading and felt that a young man was beside her and that he was sad
because she was not letting him go. I soon realized that it was my
friend George. She had heard that I had written about her son in the
French version of this book and wanted to meet me. I believe George
arranged this incredible meeting because his mother had been holding
on to him while she tried to make sure justice served for his death. He
wanted his mother to know that he had accepted the way he had died
and he wanted her to accept it too. He just wanted her to be happy
and at peace so he could be happy and at peace too. As in life, some
souls want justice and closure and other souls just want to move on.

How can we know if our loved ones are at peace? If we are at
peace, they are at peace, and vice versa. If we have difficulty accepting
their death, they will stay near us until we accept it, and if they have
difficulty accepting their passing, we will sense it too.

We can help our loved ones cross over. This can be done through
a simple conversation. It is like helping your best friend prepare for
their dream voyage. Of course they will be afraid, have doubts, and
be nervous about leaving. However, remind them that making this
trip will be worth the joy, that this journey has been planned for a
long time, and that you (and all the other people who will remain
here on earth) will be fine despite their departure. Talk to your deceased loved one, forgive them, ask for their forgiveness, thank them
for being in your life, and invite them to go into the light knowing
that you will be well. Tell them that once they are in the light, they
can return much more easily. This is the most beautiful gift you can
give your deceased loved ones.

3
MEDITATION

"Half an hour of meditation is essential,
except when you are busy. Then a full hour is needed."
—*Saint Francis de Sales*

Before we discuss how to communicate with our angels, guides, and deceased loved ones, let's take a look at meditation and how it can greatly improve our ability to connect with the other side.

Meditation is extremely beneficial for the mind, body, and spirit. It is one of the greatest tools we have at our disposal to help us heal ourselves on all levels. Meditation is known to calm our minds, heal our bodies, and uplift our spirits.

The benefits of meditation are numerous. For example, for the mind, it helps with mental strength, focus, memory, decision making, and problem solving. Emotionally, it can help with stress reduction and alleviate depression, anxiety, and worry. It also promotes well-being, calmness and serenity, confidence, and faith. And physically, it promotes health, wellness, and healing in the body.

Practicing meditation regularly will help you feel calm, centered, and peaceful, plus you will be more receptive to extrasensory information.

There is nothing complicated about meditation. Just sit comfortably in a quiet place and be with yourself. The important thing is to breathe and allow yourself to be with the inner silence. Thoughts about your problems and worries will come to mind, but just refocus your attention on your breathing. Playing relaxing music or lighting a candle or incense might help you relax. The goal is to feel calm and receptive and to feel the peace within.

A basic way to meditate is what some people call "mindful" meditation. A method for mindful meditation is given in the next section.

Let me share with you my personal experience with meditation.

For twelve years I lived with ulcerative colitis. When I was home on sick leave for an occupational burnout, I decided to stop taking the drugs so I could really feel my body and understand what it was trying to tell me. (Please note that I do not encourage you to stop taking your medication without the consent or supervision of your doctor.)

Through meditation, I discovered that I was experiencing tremendous stress. I realized I was nervous and anxious, especially when I went out in public. In fact, I felt fear. When I began to meditate twice a day for twenty minutes, the first thing I noticed was that my symptoms diminished. Meditation brought me into a state of calmness, serenity, and confidence, and I was able to remain in this state for most of the day. When I went shopping, I felt much more at peace and I no longer had to run to the bathroom. I slept like a baby for the first time in months. Within a few days, my symptoms were completely gone, as if by magic.

During the second week of my experience with meditation, I was inspired to rearrange my furniture. I had a clear vision of how I should place the furniture in my living area. So I immediately arranged a sitting area by the window with two chairs facing each other and a small table placed in between, exactly as I had seen in my vision.

This area became my favorite place in the house. I spent most of my time there. The space was uncluttered and energy flowed more freely. From one chair I could see the sunrise, and from the other I saw the sunset. I had a wonderful view of the ocean, and I could enjoy it much more after I was inspired to make this change. I wrote, meditated, and did all my personal consultations in that space.

After a couple weeks of meditating, I woke up on a Friday morning with a strong sensation of fear. My ego had taken over and I was feeling fearful. By Monday morning I had started to bleed again. That is when I understood the feelings of insecurity and fear that were causing my colitis. I felt insecure about my future. So I decided to meditate. I felt the need to connect with my soul and find peace within. It took one hour to feel peaceful. I was guided by my angels to imagine what I really wanted in my future instead of focusing on what I did not want. Imagining how I really wanted my future to be increased my feeling of well-being and my vibration. I continued to imagine my future until I felt peaceful, hopeful, even excited, and the fear dissolved.

During the third week, I was meditating one evening before going to bed to help me sleep. After about twenty minutes, I saw myself meeting a publisher for the French version of this book. I felt the urge to write him a letter requesting an appointment during my next visit to Quebec City. I got out my computer and began writing him the letter I heard dictated in my mind. The next day, with a clear head, I reread the letter and sent it to the publisher. Within one hour I received a positive confirmation for an appointment. What happened next? The book was published in French and became a national bestseller within four months.

During another meditation, I put on a relaxing melody of the ocean. At first I had trouble concentrating, but then the angels guided me to meet my spirit guide. I saw myself embark on a small boat and make my way out to an island where I was to meet my spirit guide. I saw myself get out of the boat and walk up a beach and then some stairs to this amazing white building, and there I met my guide Menerva. She was a beautiful woman all dressed in white, and she had a gift for me: a key. She told me that it was a key to access all knowledge and wisdom. We sat there for a long time discussing my life purpose and how she would help me achieve my goals. It was a beautiful experience.

These are the wonderful kinds of experiences you can have through meditation. So I encourage you to start taking time every day to sit quietly and meditate to heal your mind, body, and soul.

EXERCISE
Mindful Meditation

I recommend you meditate once or twice a day for twenty-minute periods.

Sit comfortably, with your legs crossed and your back straight. Close your eyes and focus on your breath. Spend the first couple minutes just noticing how your breath enters your body through the nose and fills your chest area and stomach. Slowly exhale and notice how the breath is exhaled through the nose and deflates your lungs and stomach. Your thoughts may wander, but keep bringing your attention back to your breath.

Next, pay attention to your body and any sensations you may be feeling, such as pain or tingling. Bring your attention to each part of your body that may be speaking to you. Notice any emotions that arise when you focus on a particular part of your body. Do not judge or think about the pain or the emotions related to the pain, but just allow yourself to feel the physical sensations and the related emotions.

Now, let go of any sensations and emotions and focus all of your attention on your third eye, the space between your two eyes and slightly above. Notice if you see any colors or shapes in this area. This is where your visions will come through. Spend at least a minute or two focusing all of your attention in this area. Then bring your attention to your ears and listen to everything going on around you. Try to listen to every little sound. Usually you might be annoyed by noises when meditating, but include these in your practice, knowing that they are helping you develop your clear hearing. Listen to things that are in the room and then listen for sounds that are farther away, outside of your home. Listen as far away as possible.

Finally, bring all of your attention into your heart and feel all the love that is there waiting for you. Sit with this feeling of love and peace for as long as possible. Send love outward toward others, and feel the love flow back to you. Imagine this love flowing out of your heart and going out into the world, and feel it flow back toward you. Allow this love to fill you up until you feel it overflowing all around you. Take a moment to be grateful for all this love and this beautiful experience.

4
HOW ANGELS
AND SPIRITS COMMUNICATE

"When a sudden inspiration takes you, it can most certainly
be of natural origin. But it is probable that more often than
we think, it is whispered in our ear by our guardian angel."
—*Jacques Maritain*

Angels and spirits communicate with us through what we call "clairs."
The word *clair* actually means "clear." There are various types of clairs,
such as *clairvoyance* (clear seeing), *clairaudience* (clear hearing), *claircognizance* (clear knowing), and *clairsentience* (clear feeling). We all
have at least one or two of these clairs naturally. Understanding which
of these clairs you have developed most will help you better receive
your messages. Other clairs exist, such as *clairgustance* (clear tasting)
and *clairalience* (clear smelling), which are associated mainly with the
communication with spirits. Sometimes we may receive an impression
of a smell, a whiff, or of a taste of something that a spirit would like
to share with us, such as the smell of tobacco or cologne or the taste
of alcohol. To help you discover and develop your gifts, we will focus
mainly on the four principal clairs.

To help you open up your clairs, I recommend the following:

- Walk in nature for at least twenty to thirty minutes a day.
- Shower upon arriving home from the office or department store.
- Meditate for twenty minutes, preferably twice a day, to remain centered.
- Eat light and reduce your consumption of sugar, alcohol, caffeine, and nicotine.
- Limit drama, such as news, social media, and violent shows.
- Avoid the use of drugs (that can attract negative energies).

This all may seem a bit drastic, but the more you are in a state of calm and receptivity, the more you will develop your attention, awareness, intuition, and connection to the divine.

Exercise is an excellent way to open your clairs. When we move, we breathe more deeply and messages can come through more easily. On more than one occasion, I have received messages for my friends while walking.

A good shower has the same effect as exercise. You have surely noticed that often the best ideas come to you during or after a shower. This is because you have cleared your energy field, which facilitates divine communication. Running water creates an electromagnetic field and generates energy, which spirits are drawn to.

Good physical and psychological nourishment can greatly help in the development of your clairs. Your clairs are related to your chakras, which are energy centers that absorb and distribute energy to different parts of your body. When you absorb too much negative energy through toxins or drama, the energy in your chakras can slow down or become blocked, and this in turn can affect the development of your clairs and your health in general.

Clairvoyance

Clairvoyance is defined as the capacity to see something that is not physically present. It is associated with the third eye chakra. We can see either outside of us, as if we are seeing another dimension superimposed on our own physical world, or we can see inside of us, in our mind's imagination. Clairvoyant people may see a clear vision outside of themselves of a real angel or spirit. They may also see a little movie running in the upper right corner of their vision, a photograph directly in front of them, flashing lights in their peripheral vision, or even words that are displayed above a person's head or a door frame as they enter a room.

When you see little flashing lights out of the corner of your eye, this denotes the presence of angels. When you turn your head toward the lights, they disappear. White lights signify the presence of angels and colored lights represent archangels.

People think that if they cannot see an angel or spirit in physical form, they must not be clairvoyant. What most people don't realize is that we can more easily see visions inside our head through our imagination, with our eyes closed. Imagination is our main connection to the divine. God, the angels, our guides, and our loved ones communicate with us through our imagination. We should never tell our children, "It's just your imagination." This diminishes the importance of that part of us that is our direct connection to the divine. Once you are used to seeing angels and spirits with your eyes closed, you can then learn, through practice, to keep the vision clear with your eyes open. If you are new to clairvoyance, I recommend practicing seeing with your eyes closed and gradually opening them once in a while, all while staying focused on the vision.

A lot of people are afraid to see. We have all seen a few horror movies in our youth, and we may have developed a fear of seeing something disturbing. Also, some people who were clairvoyant from a very young age have blocked this gift out of fear or non-acceptance by the adult world around them. Don't be afraid to see. Hold the clear intention to see only love, and that is what you will see.

I was speaking recently to another medium who believes that being less clairvoyant makes him more compassionate and able to love spirits unconditionally. He explained that he is more clairsentient and can feel spirits. He believes that because he doesn't necessarily see them, he has no judgment about them or how they look, and the feeling of unconditional love allows him to help those souls cross over into the light.

Visions

You may receive visions or images in your head that are actually messages for you or someone else. When I have a vision, it is like a photograph superimposed upon reality. My eyes are open but I see an image in front of me, like when I lived in Ontario and one morning I woke up and saw an image of my mother's face in front of me. I blinked my eyes and it was still there. I closed my eyes and could still see it. It was as if the angels were saying to me that I needed to visit my mom. So I made plans to visit her in the coming weeks for her birthday. After I called my girlfriend in Montreal and made plans for the road trip, the vision went away. It was as if I could not see anything in my future until I visited my mom. And the vision was right. After my visit, I knew in my heart that I was meant to move closer to where she lived. I had known for a while that I was going to move, but I didn't know where until I spent a week visiting my mom.

Another time, while visiting my family, I woke up one morning with a clear image of the view of the ocean from my house. To me, this message was a clear sign that it was time to return home.

Sometimes we might have a vision of our future, of ourselves doing other things. For example, during a meditation I saw myself in a hospital doing an energy treatment on a patient. A few years later, I was doing voluntary Reiki treatments at the hospital for patients with different kinds of diseases.

Always pay attention to your visions. They are surely a message for you or your loved ones.

Developing Clairvoyance

One of the best ways we can develop our clairvoyance is with our imagination. For example, spend at least a few minutes every day visualizing something in your mind, like an object or a special place you have visited. Imagine the object or place in great detail and use a lot of color. Build it in your mind's eye and this will help you with your clairvoyance. The angels say it is like polishing an instrument. When we use our imagination, we are polishing our third eye.

Speaking of the third eye, it is located between our two eyes and slightly above. This eye looks exactly like our own two eyes. We can encourage it to open by focusing our attention on it and imagining it opening.

Fear is the biggest reason why we don't see. Take out a sheet of paper and write down exactly what you are afraid of seeing. Next, say affirmations such as "I see only love," "I see clearly," and "I am extremely clairvoyant."

Also, practice being more observant. Look at everything around you as if it is the first time you've ever seen it. Notice all the details about an object or place. For example, look at the scenery in front of you and notice everything about it: the houses, their color, the textures, if the windows are open or closed, if there is a car in the driveway, if the house is well-kept or rundown, if children are outside playing and what they are playing, how they are dressed, if they are happy, etc.

I found that painting helped me look at things around me in a different way and open up my clairvoyance. Any kind of artwork will help us develop our sight, because we become more observant. When we start to imagine how we would go about drawing or painting a certain object, we look at it more closely. We observe its distinctive shape and colors and also how the light reflects off of it.

I believe many people have more clairvoyant ability than they think. For example, let's say you're wondering how you could redecorate a room in your house and you receive an image of how you should place the furniture or the color scheme that you should use. These are not coincidences. Clairvoyance is clear messages we receive in the form of visions. We can develop our clairvoyance by visualizing or imagining things. When an image pops into our mind, it is clairvoyance. If we build the image in our mind, it is visualization, but this helps open our clairvoyance.

My clairs really began to develop when I started taking Reiki classes. Reiki is a Japanese method of healing that is shared by Reiki Masters. Reiki is universal energy that we invite into our bodies in order to transmit it to another person through the use of our hands to help facilitate healing on all levels.

After taking my Level I Reiki class, it was my clairvoyance that started to develop. I was practicing on my Reiki Master and I started to see the energy in the room. It was as if I could see that every-thing was vibrating. The energy I saw resembled the heat that can be seen above the pavement on a hot summer day. It was as if all the ob-jects in the room began to speak to me. They told me that different materials, such as wood, iron, glass, and even the human body, all vibrate at different frequencies, which explains why we perceive their different textures. Everything pulses at a different rate, but there is a harmony among them. The room appeared almost surreal, like a mi-rage in the desert. I had the sensation that what I was seeing was in a different dimension. I felt a deep respect and love emanating from everything in the room, and I thanked them for the message.

Clairsentience

A clairsentient person may be distinguished by their ability to sense energy. Energy can be felt as much on the inside of the body as on the outside. Clairsentience develops from the heart chakra.

As opposed to empathy, which is the ability to relate to another's feelings, clairsentience is the ability to actually experience and feel another person's feelings and emotions in our own body. We can feel in our own body the physical as well as emotional discomforts of others. In my private readings, the first message I receive for my client or about a deceased loved one is about their emotional and physical state. Angels always explain to me what is happening on the physical and emotional levels of the person, why they are in this state, and how it can be relieved or cured.

I feel the emotions of the living and the deceased. If you are sad, I feel sad. If the deceased person feels guilty, I feel almost as if the guilt is mine. That is why, before I do a reading for someone, I always check my own personal well-being and then bring myself to a state of se-renity to be able to discern what belongs to me and what belongs to the other person. For me, being able to feel another person's physical or emotional state is a true gift. I have felt great love between couples that have been separated by death. This is an emotion that feels like a mixture of admiration, pride, respect, and unconditional love. It is a wonderful gift to be able to feel the love between two beings!

People who have highly developed feminine energy have a lot of what is called "feminine intuition" because their heart chakra is very open. They feel things; they have gut feelings about certain people or situations. Often we discount our gut feelings and end up regretting it later. If you have to make a choice in your life between two options, I suggest you sit down and imagine yourself in each option and notice the feelings you experience in each situation. The option that feels the best is generally your answer. If you feel happy, joyful, peaceful, and expectant, then that is the right choice for you. On the other hand, if you feel fearful, stressed, or sad, that is an indication that you are veering away from what God and the angels want for you. Peace is always guiding you in the right direction. Follow the path that brings you the most peace.

A clairsentient person can also feel energy on the outside of their body, like the heavy atmosphere in a room where there was a disagreement. They also feel the sudden change of temperature in a room when a soul is present.

Have you ever felt goose bumps during a conversation? This is usually a sign that the other person is telling you the truth. Have you ever felt your hair rise on your head? It can be a sign that a deceased person is near you. When I am standing in front of someone, I often feel this sensation that tells me that there is a deceased loved one around the person.

My grandfather died on Valentine's Day in 2002. He often visits me at that time of year. In 2010, I was in my office talking with my technician and I felt someone pushing me on my left side. I was sitting at my desk and there was no one next to me, but it was so persistent that I had trouble keeping my mind on the conversation. At noon, I went to lunch with the girls from the office and, not feeling very well, chose a booth in a quiet corner. I sat next to the wall so I could withdraw a bit from the conversation. I still had the sensation that someone was pushing on my left arm, but there was only the wall next to me. Finally, exasperated by all the pushing, I turned my head to the left and my eyes fell on the paper border on the wall. I could not help but smile because I knew it was my grandfather. There were tiny little houses on the wallpaper border with the words "Josephine's Boutique." Josephine is my grandmother's name.

Developing Clairsentience

Remaining aware of the state of your body and emotions can help in developing clairsentience. When you know how you feel, you can notice the difference when you are in the presence of others. When you first meet someone, are you able to sense their mood? Do you notice a difference in your own body with the arrival of the other person? Do you feel any pain that you didn't feel before? When you enter a room, notice the atmosphere. Is it heavy and negative or joyful and light? Do you develop goose bumps when listening to someone? This can be an indication that the person before you is telling you the truth. Have you ever felt the hair on your head rise or tingle? This may indicate the presence of a deceased loved one standing next to the person.

To help you develop your clairsentience, you can ask a friend for a photograph of someone they know well but you don't. Look into their eyes and notice if you feel anything about the person. How did they feel when the photograph was being taken? Notice if you can feel their emotions and maybe any physical ailments they might have had.

Another interesting exercise is *psychometry*, which is "reading" an object. All objects retain energy from their owners, so you can try this exercise with your friend's grandmother's jewelry, for example, and try to sense what she was like. Hold the object in your left hand if you are right-handed. If you are left-handed, hold it in your right. The hand with which you write is your dominant, male side and is the hand that gives energy; your other hand is the hand that receives energy and information. Close your eyes and notice if you feel any different emotions in your body, any particular sensations or pains that you don't regularly have. If the deceased grandmother passed due to a heart attack, for example, you may feel a pain in your chest near your heart. If she experienced emphysema, you may feel difficulty breathing. Also notice any changes in your emotions. Do you feel happy, sad, angry, guilty, or at peace? Through clairsentience, we can feel the person's main emotions, meaning the emotions they felt most of the time they were on earth.

I believe we are all clairsentient to a certain extent but we just don't realize it. For example, one day I had a headache and my niece Mandy came to visit me. Not more than fifteen minutes after her arrival, she said, "I have a funny headache!" I noticed that my pain was gone and she must have taken it on, because she is a very empathetic person. When this happens, thank your body for the message about the other person's state and ask Archangel Raphael to take it away for you.

When I attended the Level II Reiki class, I started to feel the pain of the person I was treating in my body. For example, I asked the lady who was lying on the table if she had a lump in her right breast. I had suddenly felt a big bump below the elastic of my bra that I hadn't feel before. She checked with her hand where I indicated to her and sure enough she felt the bump I mentioned. She went to the doctor's office a few days afterward and fortunately it was not cancerous.

Clairaudience

Clairaudience is clear hearing. We can hear music, sounds, or voices that are not usually perceptible to human ears through what we call our ear chakras. We can hear inside our head or outside of our ears.

For example, we can hear a voice either in our head or next to our ears that suggests solutions, spontaneous ideas, and clear directions in our life or answers to our questions. These voices may belong to our spirit team, such as our guide or our guardian angel. Since your dominant hand is your male side, if you hear a voice on that side it is from your guide, and if you hear a message on the other side it is from your angel.

In the province of Quebec, we have to attend college after high school if we wish to go to university or if we wish to complete a technical degree. I attended college to be a civil engineering technician. On the first day of my last year of college, I entered the main doors and clearly heard a voice whisper in my left ear one morning, "Wouldn't you like to go to university?" My first thought was, "Yes, I would love to!" But my ego immediately spoke up and said, "Another four years of school? That's a long time! And where will you find the money?" I immediately dismissed the inspired idea, but at the end of the fall session I felt compelled to apply. However, I chose not go to university that year because I loved my new job. But the following year, a series of events guided me there. I realized over the years that when the angels inspire us with an idea, it is their way of guiding us politely in the direction we need to go. We have free will. We can always choose not to listen, but this often leads to painful situations. But the angels always give us an opportunity to choose again.

Another time I heard the words "move, move, move" in a very clear and firm male voice. I was living in a beautiful apartment in Pembroke, Ontario. It was the most beautiful place I had ever lived in up until then. After teaching a workshop on angels, my new students told me they had all received the same message for me too. So against my will, I packed up all my stuff to move into a house with a friend, where I rented a room. The day I moved, my one guy friend who was supposed to help me didn't show up. Only later did I learn that his best friend's wife had given birth. So I and the lone man I had found in the newspaper to help me move loaded all my stuff into a truck and drove to my friend's house, which was much farther away from my work, in a tiny village. My friend was away, so she wasn't there to help either.

I cried the whole day and told the angels that I hoped they knew what they were doing because I didn't. After unpacking all my stuff, I stepped back and looked at the result. At that moment, I knew in my heart why I had been guided to move. I was too attached to my old apartment. Because I no longer had that apartment, I no longer needed to stay in the government job that paid for it. I felt free and I knew it was just a matter of time before the angels would guide me somewhere new.

Angels can be very persistent when they want to be. While I was living with an ex-boyfriend, I knew I was not in love, but I was waiting for the right time to leave. One evening I began to hear a voice in my head telling me, "You love him, but you're not in love!" This same phrase started to repeat itself like a mantra. The next morning, I hurried off to work lest the words jump out of my mouth. I was not ready to express them out loud. At noon, while my boyfriend was preparing lunch, the phrase started repeating so fast and so strongly in my head that I could not restrain myself any longer and I almost shouted, "I love you, but I'm not in love! I can't do this anymore!" I felt that the angels danced with joy around me. "Finally!" I thought I could hear them say.

Developing Clairaudience

One of the best and simplest ways to develop your clairaudience is to notice everything that is going on around you. For example, go for a walk and listen very carefully to all the sounds around you. Stretch your ears (in your mind) to listen for sounds. What I like to do is to start by listening really closely to my body, to the sounds that my clothes make when they rub against my body and my feet make when they hit the ground. Next, I listen to the people walking by, the bikers, the bees buzzing near me, the birds chirping in the trees, and the wind in the leaves. Then I listen a little farther away to hear the kids playing, the traffic, the sounds of sirens, a lawn mower, a plane flying overhead, or a boat speeding by in the distance. I keep stretching my ears to hear as far away as possible and then I slowly bring my hearing back to listen to my feet hitting the ground again.

Another great way to develop your clairaudience is by imagining sounds. Sit in a quiet place and imagine the sound of a guitar, coffee brewing, a helicopter, or the typing on a computer. Think of different sounds you can imagine and spend time building each sound in your head.

Meditation is another great tool you can use to help open up your clairaudience. Sit quietly and just listen to the sound of your breathing. Listen to all that is going on around you and then bring your awareness back to listening to your breath.

Claircognizance

Claircognizance is simply knowing. This knowing comes in through the crown chakra. We simply know something about someone, an object, or an event. The information just seems to pop into our head.

The information may be repeating thoughts or ideas. For example, if you lose an item and ask the angels to help you find it, its location will simply pop into your head. It shouldn't take any effort. Just allow the information to come to you. When I worked as an engineer, I often used my claircognizance at work. When I was working on a project and I got stuck, I would put it aside and take a short break. Upon my return, the solution would simply come to me. Claircognizance is very common in analytical or mentally oriented people. Engineers, scientists, accountants, and doctors tend to be very claircognizant and ironically may not even know it. Genius ideas just come to them seemingly out of nowhere.

Often we hear people say that their best ideas come to them upon waking, while in the shower, or during their exercise routine. When you take a shower, you are cleaning your energy field, which opens up the channel to receive more information. The same thing happens when you exercise or meditate. Breathing deeply opens the channel between the crown and the heart chakras, and ideas will come more easily. Inventors and entrepreneurs tend to be mostly claircognizant and can achieve great success when they follow this type of divine guidance.

So how do you know if a message is from claircognizance or ego? The messages from the angels are always based in love and not fear. A message from the angels will be inspiring, loving, and repeating. The ego will always bring you into the emotions of fear, dread, and guilt. Claircognizant information seems to be just dropped into your mind when you are thinking about something else. Thoughts from your ego usually lead you to feel negatively or bad about yourself or a situation. Claircognizance is usually wise guidance and rings true.

Claircognizant people simply know if someone is lying to them, they know if something is right or wrong, and they know who is calling when the phone rings.

For example, one day I received the message that I was going to move. As I was walking down the stairs in my house, I happened to look out toward the back yard and the *idea* spontaneously came to me that this would be my last summer in this house. I didn't hear the message, I didn't necessarily feel it, nor did I see it. I just simply knew it. I received a message that I needed to start cutting the energy cords between me and my home. I had no idea where I was going to move, but I simply knew that I would. And sure enough, the next summer I sold the house.

One day I questioned a decision that I had made a few months earlier to the point of having regrets. That evening I prayed and asked the angels for guidance as to whether I had made the right decision or if I had really missed an opportunity that I would regret all my life. The next morning, an idea came to me about a choice I had made in the past. It was the decision not to go to university immediately after college. I hadn't followed that guidance the first time, but things had fallen into place so that the following year I ended up going to an English university for two years instead of having to do four years in French. So in hindsight, having made the decision a year later turned out to be even better for me. This confirmed to me that even if I did not feel ready to seize the opportunity the first time, the angels would take care of me and a second offer would be even more appropriate for me. I had to have faith.

One Monday morning after moving to Ontario, I woke up with the idea that it was time to find a job. So I prepared my resume and business cards and toured the city all week. I visited all the engineering firms in town. I even went to a conference for entrepreneurs on safety in excavation. I gave out my business cards to several contractors and even received a call for a potential job. On Friday afternoon, something told me to go to the resource center for women on the military base. It was at least three o'clock in the afternoon when I finally arrived there. Upon entering the building, I noticed a huge billboard and there, right before me, was a poster announcing three Audit Team Leader positions. I felt my heart leap and thought, "Ah! This is the perfect job for me!" I knew without a doubt that the angels had gotten me out of bed on Monday morning just so I could see this poster. I was sure it was the job for me. Two months later, I was hired without jumping through any hoops because I was the only person who was actually qualified.

Note that when you feel your heart make a somersault accompanied by an "ah!" this is a sure sign that what you are hearing or seeing is for you. It is your soul's way of confirming to you that you are recognizing something that is destined for you. It is not envy or lust but more a recognition by your soul of a direction that was already destined for you. Accept it with grace.

So claircognizance is when you just know something. It's when an *idea* just pops into your head out of the blue. You receive a knowingness about a person, a situation, or a future event.

In my readings, I often meet people who have pain on the top of their head. The angels tell me that these people "break" their heads to find solutions to their problems when they could just simply ask the angels for help and allow the answers to come to them in the form of ideas in a claircognizant way.

Developing Claircognizance

How best to develop your claircognizance? I have found that simply asking a question and allowing the answer to come to you is one of the best ways. Once I ask a question of my angels, I get busy with other tasks and the answer just comes to me when I least expect it.

You can ask your angels to help you find something you lost and notice any repeating ideas that come to you. Don't think about it. Keep busy with anything else and just expect the answer to pop into your mind.

You can ask your angels or spirit guides to help you with your problems at home or at work and then notice any great ideas or inspirations that come to you.

Another great way to develop your claircognizance is with automatic writing. For example, I often sit with pen in hand and simply ask the angels, "What message do you have for me today?" Or you can ask for a specific answer to any question. Then just allow the answer to come to you. Don't judge or censor the message; just write whatever comes to mind, and while you are busy writing, more information will flow into you.

You can also increase your claircognizance by spending time in nature. Nature purifies your energy and allows you to receive messages much more clearly and easily. The same thing happens when exercising. Breathing deeply opens the channel of intuition. If you're exercising in nature, then it's doubly good.

Meditation is another effective method to improve your claircognizance. By being relaxed, slowing your mind, and focusing on your breathing, a candle, or your heartbeat, you can open your mind to receiving messages from the divine.

Lastly, once you receive the guidance, be sure to follow it and be grateful for the messages you receive. The more you listen, act accordingly, and are grateful, the more clear guidance you will receive.

How to Develop Your Clairs

One of the best ways to develop your clairs is by focusing on enhancing one clair per week. This will really help you be comfortable with each one of your clairs before you attempt to work with them all together. You can keep reading the rest of the book while doing these exercises.

EXERCISE
Developing Clairvoyance

At the beginning of the first week, start by sitting quietly and meditating for a few minutes. Then bring your attention to your third eye and simply feel or see if it is open. If you sense that it is closed, ask the angels to help you with opening your third eye. Say, "Thank you, my darling angels, for opening my third eye. Please remove any fears or blockages that I have that may be preventing me from seeing. Help me see only love in myself and others. I know it is safe for me to see the truth and the future. Thank you, thank you, thank you."

Practice the meditation from chapter 3 and put a lot of attention on your third eye. Just allow any colors or images to come to you and develop into form. Allow them to become clear, bright, and colorful. Also, before meditating, ask your angels, "Dear angels, please show yourselves to me in a vision so I may know that you are near me and help me develop my clairvoyance."

In addition, take time each day to practice visualizing an object or a place. Imagine as much detail as possible. Make the vision as bright and colorful as you can. You can choose a different object each day or stick with just one and focus on making it as clear as possible by the end of the week.

Each day, repeat affirmations such as "It is safe for me to see," "I see clearly," and "I am very clairvoyant."

Most importantly, practice being more observant. Go for a walk and notice everything around you. I like to start by observing what is near to me and then working my way out to the horizon. For example, I start by noticing my feet, the ground, the grass, or the snow. Notice the people walking by. How are they dressed? Do they appear happy? Notice the trees. What type of trees are they? Can you see the leaves and their shapes and colors? Do you see any birds? What types or colors are they? Look at the houses nearby. Are they all the same or what is different about them?

Lastly, take note of any visions or dreams you have.

EXERCISE
Developing Clairsentience

During the second week, you will work on developing your clairsentience and gut feelings.

Start by sitting quietly and asking your angels, "Dear angels, I invite you to come close to me so I may know that you are near me. Help me feel your presence and help me develop my clairsentience." You can ask them to touch your cheek or your shoulder or you can just close your eyes and feel their presence next to you. I often feel a gentle touch on the left side of my head when my angel is near.

During the entire week, notice all the physical sensations you have. Stay aware of your body and your emotions at all times. If you have a decision to make, notice your feelings to see if you feel good or bad, happy or tense. When you meet someone, notice if you are able to feel their mood, and also pay attention to whether something has changed in your own body because of their presence.

When you enter a room, notice the atmosphere. Does it feel heavy and dark or light and joyful? Have you noticed a cool breeze passing near you? Have you felt the hair rise on your head? This may be a sign that a deceased loved one is near. Have you felt goose bumps during a conversation? Feeling goose bumps may indicate that the person standing before you is telling you the truth.

Write down everything you notice physically inside and outside of your body.

Also ask a friend for a photograph of someone close to them whom you do not know. While staring at the photograph, look into their eyes and see if you can feel how the person may have felt while the photo was being taken. Next, notice in your own body any new sensations indicating what illnesses or diseases they may have had.

It is always fun to work with a partner or group. Exchange objects that belong to someone in your family so you can practice reading objects. Close your eyes and feel in your own body how the object's owner may have felt physically or emotionally.

Write down everything you notice physically inside and outside of your body.

EXERCISE
Developing Clairaudience

During the third week, you will focus on your clairaudience.

Sit quietly and ask your angels, "Dear angels, speak to me inside or outside of my ears so I may know that you are near me and help me develop my clairaudience." Next listen for any soft voices you may hear. This may take some practice, but with diligence and patience you will hear them.

Meditation is one of the best ways to develop your hearing. During your meditation this week, pay extra attention to everything you hear.

A great way to develop your clairaudience is to notice everything that is going on around you. For example, go for a walk and listen very carefully to all the sounds around you. Stretch your ears (in your mind) to listen for sounds. Start by noticing all the sounds that are close and work your way to listening to sounds that are very far away. Keep stretching your ears to hear as far away as possible and then slowly bring your hearing back to listen to things that are close again.

During the week, take note of anything you hear that seems to be speaking to you. What songs do you hear on the radio or what tune is playing in your head? Do the words of the chorus speak to you? Do you hear clear directions being whispered in your ear? Have you overheard a conversation that seemed to be a message for you?

Also, spend time every day imagining sounds. For example, you can imagine the sound of a train, a speeding car, a clock, an instrument, and so forth.

Note in your journal all the experiences you have with clairaudience this week.

EXERCISE
Developing Claircognizance

During the fourth week, you will work on developing your claircognizance.

You can ask your angels for help. Say to them, "Dear angels, help me develop my claircognizance and let me know that you are close to me by dropping inspiring ideas into my mind."

You can ask the angels to help you find something that is lost or help you resolve problems at work or in your personal life. Pay attention to all ideas that seem to just pop into your mind.

Notice any repeating ideas. Have you received any great ideas to help you solve your personal or work problems?

Before exercising, going for a run or a bike ride, or even jumping into the shower, ask the angels a question to which you would like to have the answer and then notice any genius ideas that come to you. Don't think about it; just allow it to come to you.

Write down in your journal any inspirational ideas you receive this week.

5
SIGNS FROM ABOVE

"Your guardian angels are continually giving you messages,
frequently through signs."
—*Doreen Virtue*

One of the most common ways that angels, spirit guides, and our deceased loved ones communicate with us is through signs and messages. They send us signs in our environment, such as coins, hearts, butterflies, birds, rainbows, words, and repeating numbers. They will use mediums such as songs, books, billboards, people, radio, and even television to send a message. They can physically show themselves to us through orbs or even in our dreams. There are no limits to the different ways they can communicate with us from the other side. They will go to great lengths to get a message to us.

It is up to each one of us to notice and interpret these signs and messages for ourselves.

Signs

Let's look at some of the different types of signs and messages we can receive from above.

Hearts

I see hearts everywhere! For years I have found heart-shaped rocks and I've seen hearts in my coffee, in the gum on the sidewalk, and in the oil spots on the street. I even had a heart-shaped blister on my foot once! I have a heart below my right eye that is made of veins and freckles, but it is indeed a heart. I believe the hearts are signs from my angels telling me "you are loved" and sometimes they mean "you need to love yourself more."

I have also noticed that the shape and orientation of the heart has significance too. In my last relationship, every heart that I saw was missing a small corner at the top right. Both times we separated, I saw a heart turned upside down. The first time this happened I was returning from a business trip in a helicopter, and as we were flying over the Moisie River in Quebec, I noticed that there was a sandbar shaped like a heart but it was upside down. That same evening I left my boyfriend. It wasn't planned. Months went by, and one day, as my eyes fell onto a picture I had hung on my office wall, it came to me that this was the first time I had ever noticed an upside-down heart in the image and that it was probably a premonition of what was about to unfold.

A few months later, I got back together with this boyfriend. Then one day, upon returning from another business trip, this time by plane, I folded the tray in front of me and there on the back of the tray I noticed a heart-shaped sticker that was placed upside down and I thought to myself, "Oh no, not again!" Yes, we separated again.

Animals, Birds, and Butterflies

Our deceased loved ones often visit us through animals that they loved while on earth. My grandfather loved birds. He fed them all the time. So it was no surprise that on the day of his funeral, we noticed two little birds flying in front of our car as we were leaving the cemetery. My family and I interpreted this sign in the same way. We believed that the birds were our two grandfathers who were happy to meet again and had sent us this sign to show us that they were together and fine.

Other deceased people choose to be represented by a butterfly. If you see a butterfly that is out of the ordinary in terms of its shape or color, it may be someone dear to you who is seeking your attention.

One day, while bicycling, I saw a huge butterfly flying through the spokes of my wheel. I would have thought that this phenomenon was simply impossible, but as I looked at the butterfly, the image of my friend's deceased aunt came to mind. She was absolutely radiant. I felt that she was comfortable and at peace. She wanted me to tell my friend that she was happy and to thank him for everything he had done for her.

Numbers

I believe that everything around us is constantly speaking to us. In 1997 I started to see numbers like 1:11 and 11:11 on the digital clock in my car. I was sure that it was no coincidence and believed that these numbers were actually speaking to me. In 2004 I discovered Doreen Virtue's *Angel Therapy* book, in which she says that angels speak to us through numbers. She explained that multiple numbers and combinations of numbers have very specific meanings.

One night I felt very anxious and afraid. I was preparing to leave my boyfriend and did not necessarily feel safe being under the same roof with him. I knew he was unhappy with my decision to end the relationship. I prayed to the angels to protect me as I prepared to sleep in the guest room. During the night, I awoke at exactly 4:44 am. The numbers 444 mean the angels are with us and we have nothing to fear. The angels wanted to confirm that they were with me and were protecting me.

Just before writing this book, I noticed the numbers 999 on several license plates. I knew that it was a sign telling me to get to work!

Images

Our angels, guides, and deceased loved ones sometimes bring us messages through images. For example, six months after my mom's partner died, there was a snowstorm. She was staying at my sister's house, and with the high winds, the house was shaking. My mother prayed to her dad and her partner that night before going to bed and asked them to protect the house during the storm. When she woke up the next morning, there was snow covering the patio door in the shape of two men that looked like her dad and her deceased partner.

Messengers

The universe always sends us the right person at the right time to help us on our path. This person may be a master, a guru, or simply a passerby. Nothing is by chance. Each person, each message, each book always arrives at the moment we need them the most.

You have surely noticed that you always find the perfect book just when you need it. You read a passage and you know immediately that it is exactly what you need to know at that time. While writing the French version of this book, I was reading a book called *I Declare* by Joel Osteen, a well-known pastor in the United States. This wonderful book was exactly what I needed at that moment. It contains thirty-one promises that we are invited to declare over our life. In brief, these messages declare that God has placed a dream in each one of our hearts, and that he is there to help us realize them. The messages in this book spoke to my heart.

Here is a passage from Day 2 of the book: "I DECLARE I will experience God's faithfulness. I will not worry. I will not doubt. I will keep my trust in Him, knowing that He will not fail me. I will give birth to every promise God put in my heart and I will become everything God created me to be. This is my declaration."

Remain open to books that simply fall from the shelves or that are suggested to you by friends. There is always an insightful message waiting for you.

Movies

Sometimes angels and spirits will speak to us through a movie or television program. The movie may resemble our life and help us to accept or free us from emotions related to a certain situation. It may even give us ideas about which path to follow. For example, you wish to change careers, so you ask the angels to show you a new line of work that might interest you. You turn on the television and all of the televisions programs seem to be about the same career.

After my father died, I rented the 2013 movie *Saving Mr. Banks*, the story of how Walt Disney obtained the movie rights to P. L. Travers's book *Mary Poppins*. In the movie, we understand that Mr. Banks was really P. L. Travers's father, who was an alcoholic. That evening I felt my father's presence very strongly. I cried incessantly and felt that my dad was saying he was sorry for all that he had done because of his alcoholism. The sadness I felt that evening was really his deep pain and anguish about all that he had done. It was a very healing movie for both my father and me.

Dreams

Dreams are another way angels, guides, and spirits can communicate with us. Dreams can be premonitions about the future or they can be a reflection of what we are living in the present. Often our angels and guides will help us understand in our dreams the emotions that we feel during the day. The emotions that we feel in our dreams are the same as those we feel in our lives. However, sometimes life can be going so fast that we have difficulty noticing them. Through our dreams, the angels will show us symbols that are meaningful and provoke emotions that are similar to what we are really experiencing. It is important to write down your dreams and look up any symbols in a dream dictionary to understand what your angels and guides are telling you.

For example, I dreamt one night that I was driving a truck and the truck just kept going faster and faster. I put my foot on the brakes, but it just wouldn't slow down. I put my two feet on the brakes and still I could not get control of the truck. I was afraid I was going to have an accident.

Next I found myself in the hull of large ship, and I was looking around thinking, "This is interesting." Then these humongous steel doors started closing in on me and I knew I had to get out or I was going to be stuck in the bottom of the ship. I turned around and saw an open window, and I ran toward it and jumped through the opening. As I was going through the window, I was surprised and relieved to see someone on the other side holding out their hands to me. I heard and felt money and stuff falling out of my pockets. I communicated telepathically to the person on the other side, "Never mind what is falling out of my pockets. Just get me out of here."

This dream was very significant, as I was in a relationship that was going way too fast for me even though I had tried to slow it down. I felt I had no control. I felt that the angels were saying to me in my dream, "There is a window of opportunity for you to leave now, and you have to jump through it and let go of what you think you might lose in the process." I did choose to leave, and I'm grateful that the angels were there to love and guide me to a wonderful new life and provide everything I needed materially and financially to be well again.

Our deceased loved ones may also visit us in our dreams. They choose to come to us this way because we are less afraid to see them in our dreams than to see them appear before us. For some people, seeing a spirit can be very disturbing. So if you wish to speak to a loved one who has passed, ask them to come visit you in your dreams. You will know it is really a visitation when the dream is very vivid and seemingly real.

Orbs

Orbs are circles of light that can appear regularly in photos or videos. Some circles of light may simply be dust, but some are really spirits. Due to the speed of digital cameras, orbs (spirits) can be caught on photographs or video. Notice that these spheres of light are often near the same people. They are very visible during spiritual conferences, religious ceremonies, and family gatherings. When they are captured on video, you can actually see the lights dancing around a person or a room.

Oracle Cards

A wonderful way to receive messages from our angels, guides, and deceased loved ones is through oracle cards. Many beautiful cards are available on the market today. Go to your nearest spiritual bookstore and find yourself a special pack of oracle cards. There are many different types to choose from, such as fairies, angels, goddesses, animals, saints, and arch-angels, to name just a few. Let your heart choose which one is right for you. Many stores will have demo packs that allow you to try them before purchasing. You can also find oracle cards on your smartphone. Many wonderful apps exist today that allow you to have your oracle cards at your fingertips whenever you feel the need to connect with your angels and guides to receive a message.

Oracle cards are an excellent and quick way to receive guidance and messages. I like to do a one-card reading every morning before I start my day.

Words

Angels and guides often use words to send us messages. When you ask for a sign, stay very open to the words you see around you. There are no coincidences. One day, while walking through Old Quebec City with my nephew Steve, we were talking about life and our dreams, and at the very same moment we noticed graffiti on the wall of a building. It said, "Don't be just another brick in the wall!" We laughed because we both knew that this message was telling us to be true to ourselves, to continue to dream, and to take the necessary steps toward the life we'd always dreamed of and not settle for less.

Another time, I was going to get my hair done. As I pulled into the parking lot in front of the mall, I saw a contractor's truck in front of me. Written on the back of his truck was, "Are you missing time?" I certainly was. This was a sure message from the angels, because I was putting too much responsibility on myself and was filling my calendar to please others. I felt like I didn't have the time to focus on what was really important to me at the time. The angels were guiding me to make time for myself and to focus on my needs and priorities.

Hearing Messages

I have come to believe that angels speak to me through songs that I hum or hear on the radio. There is always a message for me in the lyrics. I have noticed many songs over the years at particular times in my life that I felt were guiding me forward.

Often I will hear a tune playing in my head in the morning. Sometimes there are just a few words, but they are always significant. For example, one time a friend had invited me to do a dinner conference at her house. The morning I was preparing to leave home for the eight-hour drive, I asked the angels if I should give this conference because I was really exhausted. I started to hear a Christmas hymn playing in my head: "Go tell it on the mountain." Then I laughed when I realized that my friend lived in the mountains. My trip and my conference went very well. Moreover, it was that conference that inspired me to write this book.

When I lived in Ontario, I felt guided to leave my job and move. For several weeks, every time I turned on the radio in my car, I heard the song "Breakaway" by Kelly Clarkson playing. The song was nudging me to take a risk and break away from my unhappy life. I felt that this song was playing just for me. It gave me wings and gave me the courage to leave my apartment, my job, and my friends and move back closer to my family.

Several years later, I was driving down the road and was listening to this all-French radio station when out of the blue this English country song came on, "Break Up with Him" by Old Dominion. I knew in my heart that it was the angels nudging me to leave my marriage, saying that I was wasting precious time and that I was not in love with my husband. When you hear a song with a message that seems so crystal-clear, know in your heart that it is meant for you.

Another way we receive messages from our angels and guides is when we overhear a conversation that seems to be pertinent to us. A friend recently told me that one day he was walking in Old Quebec City and was talking to God about how he wanted to win the lottery. He thought it would allow him to better serve the world while meeting his financial responsibilities. At that exact moment, he heard a woman near him say aloud to her friend, "But what you gonna do with all dat money?" He knew that the message had been divinely sent to him.

EXERCISE
Noticing and Interpreting Signs

I suggest that you start looking immediately for evidence that your angels and guides are with you. You may begin by asking your angels, "Dear angels, show me clear signs that you are with me and help me see signs of your presence." Then pay attention to everything you see. Look closely at your environment and notice the signs around you. Write down everything you see. Often angels will drop feathers, coins, and the like in your path.

Take note of repeating numbers you see on your digital clock and license plates. Notice the words you see on buildings, cars, etc. Notice the shapes you see in the clouds, on the asphalt, and on rocks or pieces of wood. Look at everything more closely and see if there is a message for you. Is there a television program that speaks to you? What types of pictures are hung on the walls of the hotel room or lobby you are in? Do you see images or symbols in the ceramic tiles on your floor? Is there a message in your inbox or on Facebook that you feel is speaking directly to you?

Have you been dreaming lately? What are your dreams telling you? How do you feel in your dreams? Are they happy and light or agitated and full of fear?

Write down in your journal all you see around you and its meaning. Also take note of all your dreams and visions, as well as the symbols therein.

To better understand your messages, you can consult a dream or symbol dictionary or you can simply ask your angels for clarification. There are excellent books on the market about interpreting numbers, dreams, and symbols.

Also, if you don't already have a pack of oracle cards, I strongly suggest you purchase a special pack just for you. Your oracle cards are your connection to the divine. It is best if you are the only person who uses them. You can always purchase an extra pack to share with friends and family. I find it best to always have one special pack that has only your energy in it.

When other people use your cards, they leave an imprint of their energy in them. You can simply knock on the cards to remove other people's energy. Sound clears energy. That is why you often see spiritual people using drums, bells, and other instruments to clear the energy from a room.

I encourage you to write in your journal every day.

EXERCISE

Hearing and Listening to Messages

I also encourage you to listen for messages. Ask your angels, "Dear angels, please speak to me through messages so that I may know that you are near me." Then listen to everything around you, as well as to the lyrics that play in your head.

Take note of anything you hear that seems to be speaking to you. What songs do you hear on the radio or what tune is playing in your head? Do the lyrics speak to you? Have you overheard a conversation that seems to be a message for you? Notice your emotions when listening to songs, conversations, or television or radio programs. When you feel a sense of wonder or excitement, it is usually an indication that the message is for you.

Every day, take note of the messages you hear. For example, write down:

Date: _____

Describe what you hear: _____

_____

Interpretation: _____

_____

6

CONNECTING
WITH YOUR ANGELS

"In every little thing, there is an angel."
—*Georges Bernanos*

Most people wonder where to start when they want to meet their guardian angel in person. I have found that the best way to connect with my angel is either through a guided meditation or through what I call "divine journaling."

It is rare to have a full-blown vision of your guardian angel in front of you, but most of you will be able to see your angel in your mind's eye through a guided meditation. As with any new practice, meeting your angel may take time, devotion, and practice. You can listen to a guided meditation or you can guide yourself through your imagination.

Divine journaling is receiving or transcribing a message from your angels. There are different ways of receiving messages, such as automatic writing, which involves letting the pen write by itself, and divine dictation, where we are inspired to transcribe a message we hear or simply know; or we can simply give free rein to our imagination by drawing or describing what comes to us. When we receive messages in this way, our mind becomes busy with the drawing or writing and cannot do two things at the same time. That means it cannot think about what it receives and write it at the same time. So put the emphasis on drawing or writing to distract your mind. This will allow answers to come to you more easily.

First, let's look at an example of a guided meditation. You can guide yourself through the meditation or you can record yourself reading it out loud slowly and listen to the recording afterward when you are ready to meet your angel.

Meditation to Meet Your Angels

In order to better receive messages from your angels, it is important to free yourself from whatever may be preventing from you seeing or hearing them. Stress, fear, anger, and grief are all emotions that can prevent messages from coming to you.

Close your eyes and breathe deeply for a few minutes. Breathe in slowly and exhale slowly. Focus all of your attention on your breath. Clear your mind of all worries and thoughts. It is normal that they will keep coming back, but just return your attention gently to your breathing.

Next, imagine that you are in the basket of a hot air balloon and a guide is with you, trying to bring you to meet your angel up in the sky, but you have too much luggage for the balloon to rise. The guide asks you to leave your luggage on earth.

So throw out your suitcases of fears, sorrows, and disappointments.

Feel the balloon trying to rise a little, but you still have too much luggage. Throw down your suitcases of money, friendship, work, and relationship problems. Let go of your health problems and all of your frustrations.

Continue to empty the balloon of all your worries until you feel that you have left everything on the ground.

Feel the balloon rise gently toward the sky. Breathe in the fresh air and feel the sun on your face and a gentle breeze caress your cheek.

Feel the excitement that soon you will meet your angel. Know that he or she is waiting for you. The balloon continues to climb higher and higher through the clouds. Finally, feel the balloon pierce through the clouds, then suddenly you see your angel appear and move toward you.

Notice what your angel looks like. Is this a male or female energy? Large or small? Is he or she wearing special colors? What kind of wings do you see? What do you feel? Talk with your angel. Ask for a name and whether they have something special to tell you or have any advice to give.

If you feel the need to have more information about your message, don't hesitate to ask for clarification from your angel.

Your angel also has a gift for you. Is it wrapped? What does the wrapping look like? What do you see? Open this gift in your angel's presence to see what special gift your angel has for you.

Take time to enjoy this beautiful moment! If you are unsure about what your gift represents, take the time to ask your angel for clarification. Listen to your angel's message.

Thank your angel for this wonderful and beautiful meeting and special gift. See yourself hugging your angel and sending themlove.

See your angel retreat slowly back into the clouds and wave goodbye. Feel the love you have in your heart for them.

Your guide awaits you in the balloon and is ready to take you back to earth.

Feel yourself returning very gently. Count down slowly from ten to one.

Note that this meditation can be done with your spirit guide, God, or a deceased loved one. Just use your imagination to visit them.

Divine Journaling

Another wonderful way to start a conversation with your angel, guide, deceased loved one, or even God is through a process that I call divine journaling.

The purpose of divine journaling is to encourage your first contact with your angel, your guide, your deceased loved one, or even God by asking them a question. Start by inviting them to come near you. Take the time to see if you can feel their energy around you and then receive a message.

For this exercise, I recommend that you sit in a quiet place where you won't be disturbed for at least twenty minutes.

Start by saying, "I surround myself with Archangel Michael's beautiful protective energy. I invite my angel (guide, deceased loved one, or God) to join me for this divine communication."

Next, write down a question, such as "What message do you have for me today?"

Write down what you receive in a notepad or a journal.

Relax and breathe deeply. Sometimes it helps to close your eyes at first until you receive the first messages. They may seem like thoughts to you, but write down any words or messages you receive and you will notice that it will begin to flow.

You may also feel their presence. Your angel is usually on your left side and your guide on your right. Be patient; this may take several minutes and maybe even several attempts. Don't worry and don't give up. Have confidence in your abilities and faith that your angels want to get a message to you. Just breathe deeply, let go, and stay open to anything you receive. You may or may not feel your angel's presence, but you should receive a message. Everyone is different and we all receive our guidance in different ways. Notice your thoughts and feelings and any visions that seem to pop up in your head, even any sounds you hear inside your head or around you.

Stay focused on your question: "What message do you have for me today?" Breathe deeply and check all your senses.

Do you feel a presence around you? Do you feel a change in temperature in the room? Do you feel a tingling sensation on your head or by your side? You may simply feel a loving energy by your side.

Next, ask, "Who are you?" or "What is your name?" Remember, you are always protected by Archangel Michael, so there is no reason to be afraid.

What do you feel in your body? Do you feel any emotions?

What do you see? Do you see any pictures or movies?

What do you hear? Do you hear words or a dictation?

What do you know? Are there any repeating ideas?

Write down what you feel, see, hear, and know. Be sure to check all of your senses. Note the colors and images you see, the ideas that come to you, sounds that you hear, or emotions that you feel. If you are artistic, you can use coloring pencils; this can help with the reception of ideas and messages.

Write or draw the first thing that comes to mind. Remember that analyzing or judging the message can block the process. When you start to write or draw, you will notice that the message continues to come in as if by magic, because your mind is busy transcribing and cannot analyze it.

Remember to be grateful at the end of this beautiful experience.

It can be interesting to observe how the energy may feel different between your angel, your guide, your deceased loved one, and even God.

If you don't succeed the first time, don't worry. Practice every day. You can also ask the angels for a sign during the day. You can even ask for a very specific sign, such as "If you are near me, show me _____ (three pennies, a white feather, etc.)."

When I practice this exercise, I usually get a message in the form of a dictation because I am very claircognizant, which means I just know what they are trying to tell me. While I transcribe the message, I have no time to think about it because it comes in very quickly and I don't focus on my penmanship as long as it is readable.

Ego or God

People often ask how they can know for sure if a message is from God/angels/guides or their ego. If the message starts with the word "I," it is your ego speaking to you. If, on the other hand, the message starts with something like "Dearest one" or "Dear _____ (your name)," know it is from the divine. Angel messages are always loving, positive, encouraging, and repeating. Messages from your ego are always based in fear and are critical, negative, and judgmental.

EXERCISE
Connecting with Your Angels

Meditation

I suggest that you practice the Meditation to Meet Your Angels described earlier in this chapter and imagine connecting, one at a time, with your guardian angel, your spirit guide, a deceased loved one, and God.

Take note of the special messages and gifts each one offers you. Also notice how they look and feel. During each meditation, practice each one of your clairs; what do you see, hear, feel, and know?

Notice the difference in their messages and their energies. Notice where you sense their presence: is it on the left, the right, or in front of you? Notice if they are male or female, tall or short, what they are wearing, and even how their voices or messages might be different.

Noticing how you perceive them differently will help you recognize who is with you when they show up in your life in everyday experiences.

Divine Journaling

Divine journaling is a wonderful way to start your day. I recommend that you make time every day to have a conversation with a member of your spirit team.

I suggest you communicate with your angel the first week, your spirit guide the second week, a deceased loved the third week, and God the fourth week. Focusing on just one energy for a whole week will help you get a good sense of their energy and how they communicate with you. Here are a few sample exercises for you to practice.

Meeting Your Angel Through Divine Journaling

The purpose of this exercise is to connect you with your angel. You will invite your guardian angel to come near you to receive a message.

For this exercise, sit in a quiet place where you won't be disturbed for at least twenty minutes.

Start by saying, "I surround myself with Archangel Michael's beautiful protective energy. I invite my angel to join me for this divine communication."

Your angel may feel like a male or female energy. If you are clairsentient, you will feel their energy on your left side. If you are more clairvoyant, you may see an image of them. If you are clairaudient, you might begin to hear their voice, and if you are more claircognizant, you will just know they are there and what they want to say. Be patient; it may take several minutes. Don't worry. Breathe deeply, let go, and stay open. When you feel your angel's presence, ask for a message.

Start by feeling your angel's energy. Then ask, "Who are you? What message do you have for me today?"

Notice what you feel, see, hear, and know. Tune in to all your senses. Notice the colors and images you see, the ideas that come to you, the sounds you hear, and the emotions you feel.

Remember to thank your angel at the end of this beautiful meeting.

If this exercise is not successful the first time, don't worry. Practice every day. You can also ask your angel for a sign during the day. You can even ask for something specific, such as "If you are near me, show me _____ (pennies, a white feather, etc.)."

EXERCISE
Meeting Your Spirit Guide

Follow the same steps as the previous exercise. Begin by saying, "I surround myself with Archangel Michael's beautiful protective energy, and I invite my guide to present himself (or herself) to me."

You should feel your spirit guide on your right side. Start by feeling their energy.

Notice the difference between the energy of your angel and that of your guide. Then ask, "Who are you? What message do you have for me today?"

Notice what you feel, see, hear, and know. Tune in to all your senses. Notice the colors and images you see, the ideas that come to you, the sounds you hear, and the emotions you feel. Also notice the subtle differences between the message you received from your angel and the one from your guide.

Remember to thank your spirit guide at the end of this beautiful meeting.

EXERCISE
Connecting with Your Deceased Loved One

The purpose of this exercise is to connect you with a deceased loved one. You will invite your loved one to come near you, and you will receive a message from them.

For this exercise, sit in a quiet place where you won't be disturbed for at least twenty minutes.

Say, "I surround myself with the beautiful protective energy of Archangel Michael, and I invite _____ (name of your deceased loved one) to present himself (or herself) to me in this beautiful energy."

Start by feeling the energy of your loved one. If you're right-handed, your paternal relatives will be on your right side and your maternal relatives will be on your left side. All other spirits will be on your left side. (If you are left-handed, it will be reversed.) Notice that the spirits who are less closely related to you by blood will feel farther away from you, possibly a few feet away.

Notice the differences between the energies of your angel, your guide, and your deceased loved one. When you feel your loved one near you, ask for a message.

Notice what you feel, see, hear, and know. Tune in to all your senses. Notice any colors and images you see, the ideas that come to you, the sounds you hear, and the emotions you feel.

Don't forget to thank your deceased loved one for the message at the end of this beautiful communication.

EXERCISE
Connecting with God

Follow the same steps as in the previous exercise. Begin by saying, "I surround myself with the beautiful protective energy of Archangel Michael, and I ask God to present himself (or herself) to me in this beautiful energy."

Start by feeling the energy of God. Do you feel it in front of you, beside you, or around you?

Notice the differences between the energies of your angel, your guide, your deceased loved one, and God. When you have felt God's energy, ask for a message.

Notice what you feel, see, hear, and know. Tune in to all your senses. Notice the colors and images you see, the ideas that come to you, the sounds you hear, and the emotions you feel. Also notice how the message from God may sound different. For example, is the message from God more direct and firm compared to the message from your angel, which might be more soft and loving?

Don't forget to thank God for the message at the end of this beautiful communication.

EXERCISE
Develop Your Clairs While Connecting with Your Entourage

Once you've completed the previous exercises, you can begin another month of communicating with the members of your "entourage"—that is, your angel and spirit teams—and try out different ways of receiving messages.

For example, during the first week, when you are talking to your angel every day, try using a different clair. Let them know what you are trying to accomplish by saying, "Dear angel, please help me develop my clairvoyance today." Then focus only on what you see. Just allow a vision to come to you, then write or draw any messages you receive through your clairvoyance. Do not force anything. The next day say, "Dear angel, please help me develop my clairsentience today." And so on. For example:

First week: Angel

+ Monday: Clairvoyance (sight)
+ Tuesday: Clairsentience (feeling)
+ Wednesday: Clairaudience (hearing)
+ Thursday: Claircognizance (knowing)
+ Friday: Clairgustance (taste)

- Saturday: Clairalience (smell)
- Sunday: Simply allow a message to come through all of these clairs.

Repeat these exercises the following weeks with your spirit guide, a deceased loved one, God, different archangels, and even ascended masters.

Just trust whatever comes to you. Do not judge or analyze the messages; simply transcribe them.

Remember, the mind can focus on only one thing at a time, so it cannot think about what it receives and write it down at the same time. So put the emphasis on drawing or writing to distract your mind. This will allow answers to come to you more easily. Have faith in your abilities.

I explain to my students that we all have psychic abilities, just like we can all draw. Some people feel they can only draw a stickman and others are meant to be artists, but basically we can all draw something. It is the same with psychic ability. We have to practice, practice, and practice. A guitarist becomes excellent with practice, and we can all be more proficient at using our psychic abilities if we put in the time and effort.

7

MANIFESTING
WITH THE ANGELS

"Life in itself is an empty canvas.
It becomes what you paint it.
You can paint misery or you can paint joy.
This freedom is your glory."
—Osho

God and the angels want to please you. They want you to be happy and fulfilled and live the life of your dreams. They tell me they are ready to fulfill all of your desires, but it is up to you to receive what you want. When you are ready to receive, you will receive. God gives at the moment the desire is in your heart.

The time it takes for your desire to manifest in your life sometimes depends on you and not the angels and God. It is up to you to prepare yourself to receive what you want. Be sure that your desire is really from the heart and not only in your mind. God and the angels want to fulfill the desires that stem from your heart. If you find that your desire is taking time to materialize, it may be that it is not in your best interest at this time or maybe they have something better in mind. Sometimes we can be grateful for unanswered prayers.

It could also be that you feel unworthy and the energy that you are projecting might be preventing your desire from manifesting.

We all wonder at times if someone is really listening to us. People say, "I prayed and prayed again and nothing happened!" I, too, used to feel like this in the past, until I really learned how to pray.

According to some dictionaries, praying also means to implore, to beg, to ask with supplication. Our current system of beliefs may have taught us that we are not worthy. This is false. We do not need to beg or implore to be heard. Simply choose, ask, allow, and be grateful. When we beg or plead, is it like saying to God and the angels that we are not worthy or that we do not believe they shall heed our prayers. We are living in fear.

We are also conditioned to feel guilty about praying, asking, or desiring something for ourselves. The angels want you to know that because you have free will, they cannot help you unless you ask.

In a recent consultation, the angels suggested that we pray for others and also ask others to pray for us. They said that when we pray for ourselves, sometimes we do not feel worthy and can block the manifestation of our desire; but if someone else prays for us and they really believe that we are in need, their prayers may divert our feelings of unworthiness.

It is important to know that you are certainly not a victim of your life but are the creator of it. Life manifests itself continuously, and it is up to us to manifest a positive and serene life that is in accordance with God's divine plan. The first steps are usually the hardest. Knowing what we want, feeling deserving of it, and believing that it is even possible is the most difficult part. Anything is possible once it is clear to us what we would like to experience and we feel deserving of it and believe in the possibility of our prayers being answered and the angel's capacity to deliver.

To manifest your desires in life, you need the following:

+ Worthiness
+ Desire
+ Trust
+ Imagination
+ Gratitude

Worthiness

You are made in the likeness of God, who is the divine Creator. Therefore, you are also a divine creator. The angel's say that if your life is not what you want it to be, know that on some level, possibly unconsciously, you have created it to be this way. Maybe you feel you don't deserve any better. I know that when I felt stuck in my life, it was mainly because I felt unworthy of having something better. Unworthiness prevents our desires from manifesting or our life from changing.

You are a divine Creator.

For example, if, when you were young, you felt less than others because you were adopted, you were an "accident," or you were abused, abandoned, rejected, or humiliated, you may feel unworthy. The angels want you to know that no matter how you were born, you were not an accident. God does not make mistakes. In his eyes, you are perfect, no matter what you have done or experienced in your life. You are worthy of the love and grace of God and the angels simply because you exist. Nothing can affect the love they have for you.

If you experienced any kind of situation that made you feel like you were not lovable or good enough, you may keep attracting those same kinds of situations until you feel and know in your heart that you are worthy of better. A child who is abused by her parents often will attract partners who will continue to abuse her until she decides she is worthy of better. I learned through therapy that I was lovable even though I experienced abuse. The abuse was only an event; it is not who I am. When I understood that I was a victim of an abuser, I could let go of the shame and guilt I felt. I understood that no matter what I lived, God and the angels love me anyway and their love for me is unconditional.

If you feel unworthy, the angels suggest you look at what may be preventing you from feeling worthy of their love and goodness and then build your self-esteem.

Look in the mirror and say, "Even if I was _____, I am lovable and worthy of God and the angels' goodness."

Self-Esteem and Self-Confidence

Make a list of everything you do not like about yourself, and for each item on your list, look in the mirror and tell yourself with LOTS of love, "Even if you _____, I love and accept you anyway!"

Sometimes situations or circumstances we have experienced have affected our self-confidence. We can build our own self-confidence by doing little things every day that are in line with our true selves and by celebrating our accomplishments.

The angels suggest we look at how we can love ourselves more. For example, make a list of everything you can do to be more loving toward yourself.

Also, make a list of all of your accomplishments, then look in the mirror and tell yourself, "I am so proud of you! I am so proud of all of your accomplishments. You are a strong, beautiful, courageous, and resilient spiritual being, and I am proud to be part of you and your life."

The angels tell us that it is important to love ourselves to feel worthy of God and the angels' goodness. How can you love yourself more? Here are some ideas.

+ Be impeccable with your words and thoughts. Do not criticize yourself or others. Replace these negative thoughts with words of love, such as "I am beautiful and I love myself! I am perfect just as I am! I am enough! Even though I _____, I love myself anyway!"

+ Become the best person possible, but do not be a doormat or a scapegoat. Love yourself enough to stand your ground. Learn to be assertive.

+ Be patient, nice, kind, generous, and lovable. Above all, be honest and genuine.

+ Forgive yourself.

+ Take care of your appearance and your body.

+ Take care of your home, your clothes, and your car. Everything is a reflection of you.

+ Fulfill your greatest dreams.

+ Smile.

Know that you are a divine child of God. You deserve all the love, health, and abundance that exists in the universe. In fact, this is your birthright. Worthiness begins with self-acceptance. Love and approve of yourself. You are worthy of God's goodness! Open your arms and your heart to receive it!

You are worthy of God's goodness!

Desire

Your will is God's will, so you must know what you want in life. I've learned that even though our ego may want the big job with the big paycheck to pay for all the material things we desire, God and the angels want to respond to our heart's desires, such as the need to make a difference in the world. We must always look into our heart to see what our soul really desires, because those are the needs, desires, and dreams that God and the angels wish to answer. If they answer the desires of our ego, it is usually because we need to learn an important lesson about what is truly important and will make us happy.

Know what you desire in your heart.

A practical exercise to show the angels what you really desire is to make a collage or a vision board of things that represent your dream life. The angels suggest you start by deciding what you would like your life to be. Feel from the depths of your heart what your soul truly desires. What our soul mostly desires is to make a difference in the lives of others, to be of service and live out our passion.

So first take a look at what you would like to contribute to the world. What dreams and passions do you have? Cut out images from magazines that represent those passions and what you would like to accomplish. Next, find pictures of other people who inspire you and are making their own difference in the world. Also, think about what things you would like to experience, what places you would like to visit, and what your dream home and career might look like. Would you like to get married? Have children? Make a collage to show the angels what you really desire in life. Even if a picture is worth a thousand words, I find that adding words to the collage really helps state what you really desire. So find inspiring words that speak to you and add them to your vision board.

Imagine how you want to feel and what you would like to do or achieve in your life. Do not put all the emphasis on acquiring material things. Material things will come if you do what your soul really wants you to do. You can start by making a small collage to put on your refrigerator or you can even paint your vision board.

Trust

You must be open to all possible answers to your prayers. In other words, let go and trust. Leave the "how" up to your angels and God. That is their specialty. Trusting also means having confidence that your prayers have been heard and that God and the angels are already working on them.

Do not worry about *how* things will happen. Have absolute faith that the divine is answering your prayer. Take small guided steps toward what you want. You have learned to see, feel, hear, and know the signs. So now, follow them. Make a phone call, tour potential houses, or look for a job. Taking guided action is not the same as controlling. If you are feeling impatient, you are probably wanting to control. Stay in a state of calm and receptivity to allow your dreams to come true faster.

The angels tell me that the biggest reason why our prayers seem to go unanswered is because we do not trust; we lack faith. We ask for help and then we try to control everything. Have you noticed that when you are at your wits' end, when everything seems to be going wrong, when you say, "Okay, I give up!" everything seems to work out like you want? This is when the angels cry out, "Finally! Now we can get to work."

Our responsibility is to determine what it is we desire and leave the how to God and the angels. It is best when what we desire is in line with the desires that God and the angels have for us too.

For example, let's say you would like a new home. Imagine the general important features you would like for the home and how you would feel in this new home. Do not ask for the money to buy it or for the employment to provide you with the money. Simply ask for the home. You may inherit a house, win it, or receive it in a way you cannot even imagine! Allow God and the angels to be creative in answering your prayers. Stay open to the possibilities and trust. Do not limit their imagination!

Do not limit the imagination of God and the angels.

Many people pray for help and then spend their time fretting about how to solve the problem themselves. During my private consultations, the angels tell me that we must let go, move out of their way, and trust them. They know what they are doing. Once the request has been made, we must stop thinking about it. We must refocus our thoughts whenever we find ourselves thinking about a solution. The angels suggest that we stay busy, but do not take action unless we feel divinely guided to do so. We must trust that our prayers are being answered even if we cannot see it yet. All things are possible with God and the angels, so we should remain calm and centered in faith and gratitude.

The angels tell me that we must have absolute faith in the manifestation of our desires. Everything already exists in the spiritual world; it is only a matter of time before our desires manifest in our everyday reality. The more receptive and calm we are, the faster our dreams will come true.

You must have the conviction that your beloved exists, that a state of perfect health exists, that your dream job exists, that whatever it is you dream of already exists.

Native Americans believe in what they call the "Field of Abundance." It is a place where abundance resides, where all that is desired or necessary already exists. When there is a need for a cure, a desired object, or a dream for the future, it already exists in the Field of Abundance. It is up to us to let it come to us, and we can accomplish this by believing that it already exists and that we are worthy of it. Therefore, we must remain in a state of gratitude and receptivity.

The angels say that you can purchase a box and write on the cover "Field of Abundance" and then fill it with your desires. This way, you can see that they already exist and that it is only a matter of time before they materialize in your life.

Imagination

Using our imagination is one of the fastest ways to achieve our dreams, because when we imagine what we want, we feel the emotions that attract our desires to us. This is the Law of Attraction. Children use their imagination when they play and they pretend to live the life of their dreams. When a little girl plays with her doll, she imagines she's a mother, she pretends. The little boy imagines himself driving a truck and he also pretends.

We must unleash our imagination. The angels say it is better to show them what we want instead of just saying it. The imagination—daydreaming—is more comprehensive than visualization because it includes the emotions as well as an image.

Imagination is not only what we use when we play in kindergarten; it is also our primary means of communication with the spiritual realm.

To better manifest our soul's desire, the angels recommend that we imagine and feel what we really want as if we were already living it or already had it.

Set aside time every day to imagine the life of your dreams and pretend you are already living it.

Do you want to lose weight? Pretend that you've already lost it. How do you feel? Do you feel healthy and fit? Do you eat less and better? Do you move more? Do what you would do if you had already lost the weight. Do you feel happy to be thinner? Do you feel better? How does being slimmer affect you at mealtime? Do you gulp down your food or do you savor every bite with delight? If you were already thinner, would you eat less and better? Start now and pretend; eat less and better and with more pleasure.

Do you want to be in love? Pretend that you already are. Act as if your beloved is already in your life. Talk to them when you wake up in the morning. See yourself making them breakfast. Stroll through the park with your imaginary lover. Light candles in the evening and feel the love in your heart that you feel for your beloved. Pretend that your beloved is near you when you walk, eat, or sleep. Do the things you would do if you were with your beloved. Go for a carriage ride and pretend that your beloved is with you. How do you feel? Spend time every day imagining your beloved by your side and feel how it makes you happy. Pretend that you are in love, that your beloved is with you sharing your adventures, your successes, and your sorrows.

When you pretend, you show God and the angels not only what you want but, more importantly, how you want to feel. The happiness that you feel when you imagine what you want is exactly what will help you attract your desires more quickly. If you are happy, you will attract great things. If you are unhappy, you will attract things on that same energy level. So do things to help you feel happy and fulfilled in order to attract the things that make you feel more happy and fulfilled .

Gratitude

Always be grateful for the fulfillment of your prayers in advance, because from the moment they appear in your heart, they are answered in the spiritual world.

Here are some examples of prayers:

+ "Thank you, God and my dearest angels, for finding me the perfect house!"
+ "Thank you, God and my dearest angels, for bringing me the perfect beloved!"
+ "Thank you, God and my dearest angels, for helping me realize my deepest desire to improve the lives of others!"
+ "Thank you, God and my loving angels, for helping me realize my greatest desire to _____. Thank you, thank you, thank you!"

I like to repeat the words "thank you" three times. I feel this anchors the energy of gratitude.

Always be grateful to God and your angels. The more you are grateful, the more signs and messages you will receive from them and the quicker your prayer will be answered.

I start each day by being grateful to God and the angels for their presence in my life. I thank them for all that exists in my life, such as my parents, my family, my friends, my home, my environment, my roof, my food, and my clothes.

When I worked in a government office, I gave thanks every day for my wonderful job, my super colleagues and clients, and all the wonderful opportunities that were presented to me.

Whenever doubt creeps in about your request, simply replace that thought with gratitude. Say, "Thank you for taking care of my request. I know that everything is perfect and is working out for my highest and greatest good and that of others. Thank you, thank you, thank you."

Faith

Faith is something you have to build over time. When I look back at my life, I can see that each time I needed something, it showed up. Each time I listened to the guidance, I was rewarded. I have faith that everything is always working out for my highest good. God has always been there for me and always will be.

When you have doubts that your prayer will be answered, you push away the manifestation of your desire and it takes more time to materialize. The more absolute faith you have, the faster your desire will come to pass.

I had a friend who wanted to sell a property for more than a year. She said laughingly, "I asked, but it doesn't work! I think they don't understand my accent." I believe the reason her building wasn't selling is because she didn't really believe it. She was living in fear. She didn't trust the process. Sitting in my living room, I recommended that she imagine the building was being sold. I asked her how it made her feel. She told me she felt free and happy, so I suggested that she stay in that state of emotion and avoid returning to fear. Not long after, the building was sold.

Practice with small requests. Once, at the last minute on New Year's Eve, I decided that I wanted to go out and have fun. I was told that the event I wanted to attend was sold out, so I said to my angels, "I don't know how you will do it, but I would really like to go to this place to celebrate New Year's Eve. Thank you for finding me tickets!" Less than twenty minutes later, the phone rang and my tickets were confirmed.

Our life is created from our beliefs. If we believe that we can achieve something, we will. If we believe that we are not worthy and we do not deserve something, this belief will be true too. I believe that God and the angels want what is in my highest and greatest good and will do everything they can to make me happy.

Believe that you are worthy to receive the grace of God and the angels and you will see miracles occur in your life.

Prayer for Manifesting Your Desires

Here is a sample prayer that you can say in order to help you manifest your desires.

Worthiness

"Lord God, I am worthy of your goodness, your grace, and your blessings. I know that my will is your will and you only want what is best for me."

Desire

"Dearest angels, what I really desire in my life is _____."

Trust

"My dearest angels, I trust you completely. I know you have heard my request and you are already working on its fulfillment. I promise you, my dearest angels, that I will follow your divine guidance."

Imagination

Reserve at least ten minutes a day to imagine what it is you desire in life and pretend you already have it.

Gratitude

"Thank you in advance, Lord God and my dearest angels, for the fulfillment of my greatest desire, _____ (state your desire), only if it is for my highest and greatest good and that of others. Thank you, thank you, thank you."

EXERCISE
Manifesting with the Angels

God and the angels want to please you. They want you to be happy and fulfilled and live the life of your dreams. They are ready to fulfill all of your desires, but it's up to you to receive what you want. Your prayer is answered the very moment it is in your heart.

These next exercises will help you prepare to receive an answer to your prayers.

Let's go through the different steps to manifesting.

To manifest your desires in life, remember the following: worthiness, desire, trust, imagination, and gratitude.

Worthiness

In order to feel completely worthy, the angels suggest you work on your self-esteem and self-confidence and invite you to take a look at everything that might be affecting your self-esteem and self-confidence.

For example, you may feel less worthy if you were adopted, were an "accident," or were rejected, abandoned, humiliated, abused, assaulted, etc., by a parent, mentor, or lover. Know that if an experience makes you feel shame or guilt, you may be a victim of abuse or violence.

You also may be being too hard on yourself about your past failures, your looks, or your education or lack thereof. We are often our own worst enemy.

Make a list of everything that you do not like about yourself or that makes you feel less lovable. Archangel Raphael's energy is emerald green, and he suggests we use a green pen whenever we desire to heal a certain part of ourselves.

For each thing on your list, look in the mirror and tell yourself with LOTS OF LOVE, "Even if you _____, I love and accept you anyway!"

Sometimes situations or circumstances we have experienced have affected our self-confidence. We can build our own self-confidence by doing little things every day that are in line with our true selves and by celebrating our accomplishments.

The angels tell us that it is important to love ourselves to feel worthy of their goodness. How can we love ourselves more?

Make a list of everything you can do to love yourself more. Make a list of all of your accomplishments. And look in the mirror and tell yourself, "I am so proud of you! I am so proud of all of your accomplishments. You are a strong, beautiful, courageous, and resilient spiritual being and I am proud to be part of you and your life."

Desire

The angels invite you to look into your soul to know what it is you truly desire.

Describe in your journal the life you want to live. Write it as if you are already living it in the present.

Also, find pictures and words that represent what you want to live and make a collage or vision board. You can start by making a small collage to put on your refrigerator, or you can even make a vision board that represents your whole life.

Trust

Know that the angels are already working on answering your prayers. Remain open to all possible answers to your prayers. Leave the "how" to your angels. They know how to manifest your desires. Don't worry about how things will fall into place. Have absolute faith that the divine is working out the details. Focus on taking small guided steps to move toward what you want. You have learned how to see, feel, hear, and know the signs. Now it is time to follow them.

Note any actions you feel guided to take.

Imagination

The angels tell us that using our imagination is one of the fastest ways to achieve our dreams. Set aside time every day to imagine the life of your dreams and pretend you are already living it.

What is your greatest desire?

While you are imagining this great new life, describe in your journal exactly how you would feel over the course of a full day now that your dream has come true.

Remember that most people think, "I will be happy when _____," but it is more important to be happy today just because. The joy you have in your heart today will attract and create the happiness you will experience in the future. Happiness cannot be put off until we achieve something. We must be happy first and then the achieving will take care of itself.

Gratitude

The angels suggest that we always be grateful for the fulfillment of our desires in advance, because from the moment they appear in our heart, they are answered in the spiritual world.

Saying "thank you" in advance is like saying to the divine that you have faith that your prayers will be heard and answered.

State what you are grateful for: "Thank you, God and the angels, for _____. Thank you, thank you, thank you!"

Repeating the words "thank you" three times anchors the energy of gratitude.

8
LIFE WITH THE ANGELS

"Make friends with the angels, who though invisible are
always with you.... Often invoke them, constantly praise
them, and make good use of their help and assistance in all
your temporal and spiritual affairs."
—*Saint Francis de Sales*

For most of my life, I felt a divine presence guiding me. During the
times when I felt alone, I noticed that it was me who had forsaken
what I call God and the angels and not the other way around. The
divine was always there, like electricity in the wall, ready and available. God and the angels have constantly been there waiting patiently
for me to ask for their guidance.

Have you ever had an inspiration to write a book or a play, take
a class, or start your own business and you thought, "I'm not good
enough, not smart enough, or unable to make a difference in the
world." This is your ego speaking. Your ego always makes you feel
fearful and small, and stops your momentum. God and the angels,
on the other hand, are always loving and encouraging. They say,
"Write a book," "Take a course," "Be self-employed." They want you
to be happy as you pursue your dreams. Don't be afraid to take risks.

Always listen to your divine guidance. Know that they only want what is best for you. They want you to succeed and be happy.

God and the angels want to be part of your life. They are already there next to you. You may have had a brief glimpse of their presence at some point in your life when you felt "lucky" to find the right job or meet the right person or when a dream came true. This feeling of "luck" can be part of your everyday life if you invite the angels to accompany you on your path.

Imagine how enjoyable and gratifying your life would be if you always made the right decision at the right time, if you allowed your life to be guided by your angels. Life is supposed to be fun and easy, and it can be with the help of your angels.

Have you noticed that for the most part when you are unhappy it is because you didn't follow their guidance? We know in our gut that we should run the other way, take another direction, not enter a place, or not continue a relationship, but sometimes we dismiss these feelings. And when we do, we usually end up learning some important lesson, like loving and respecting ourselves more or listening to and following our intuition.

Make it a habit to talk with your angels every day. Ask them for their advice and notice how your life can be different with their help. There is no request too big or too small for them. For example, I once asked them for help with my exercise program. I had bought a pilates video series and needed divine encouragement. I was using the beginner's exercise tape for two weeks when one morning my VCR ate the tape. I couldn't believe it! And then it came to me that I had received the encouragement I had asked for. It was a sign to proceed to the next level. Our prayers are always answered, just not always in the way we expect. You must keep an open mind and a sense of humor with the angels!

Talk to your angels about everything that is happening in your life. You will see that everything will go like clockwork if you listen. The angels are always there and always have been. It's simply a matter of perception. The more you notice and follow the signs, the more you will receive. The angels will be delighted that you invited them to help you in your life. Give them a chance to show you what they can do for you.

Decorating with the Angels

Angels love to decorate and beautify our lives. I have often seen the proof of this. I have learned over the years that we should always go with what speaks to our heart. In fact, when we experience a sense of "love at first sight," it is really our clairsentience speaking to us. When we feel our heart stir when shopping, this is a sign that this find is for us. We don't usually regret those kinds of purchases. We only regret the ones that we think we might use or the ones we purchase because we are trying to be frugal. The angels tell me that we must allow ourselves to receive if we want them to continue to bring us abundance. Don't think but feel when you are shopping. Also remember to always be reasonable. Respect your budget and pay attention to your ego. Usually when the angels guide us to purchase something, we already have the money for it, not credit but cash.

The angels encourage us to pay attention to our heart and thus our feelings. If something speaks to your heart, don't hesitate. Your mind will say, "Where do you think you will wear that?" but trust the feeling. I once walked by a store and saw a dress that just spoke to me. It looked like it would fit me perfectly. My heart skipped a beat as I saw it. Then my ego piped up and said, "Where do you think you'll wear a dress like that?" I didn't buy the dress that day, but the following week I was asked to officiate a wedding and that dress was perfect for the occasion. So I went back to the store and the dress had been sold. Luckily I was able to order another one in my size and receive it before the ceremony.

Angels want to please us. They know what we need before we know it ourselves. If we learn to listen to their gentle nudges, we will be guided to all kinds of wonderful findings and opportunities.

The angels love to embellish our lives. We can even decorate our homes with their help, without forcing anything, just following their divine guidance. We don't necessarily need to hire a decorator; we just need to follow the signs. Ask your angels to inspire you and they will find a way to communicate what is best for you. For example, you will find a picture of a room you love in a magazine, you will recognize the "great find" in the store, helpers will be readily available, and you will see that everything will fall perfectly into place.

When I started the Reiki classes, I decided to buy myself a Reiki table. So I looked on the Internet and found a man in the Gatineau area who made them. I called him on a Friday night to see if he had any in stock and he said yes, so we made an appointment to meet the next morning. I brought a friend along with me on Saturday morning and we went to his home. When we arrived, he had a beautiful purple table set up in the entrance of his basement where he kept all of his massage tables. I wanted to see them all! There were tables in all sorts of beautiful colors: navy blue, cranberry red, emerald green, and a beautiful purple. I finally decided to go with the red table because I thought it would match better with my apartment, which was painted a creamy white with nice light-green moldings.

That night, I slept in Gatineau at a friend's home, and the next morning when I woke up, I saw the color purple. I closed my eyes and I saw purple. When I opened them again, I saw the word "PURPLE." I found it strange. I went to brush my teeth and noticed a purple toothbrush, a purple toothbrush holder, and even a purple shower curtain with green and gold accents.

I went downstairs for breakfast and the purple idea would not leave me. I told my friends that I had to return the red table and exchange it for the purple one. I called the guy and he was not surprised at all. He knew that the purple table was meant for me; it was the one that he had placed in his entry for me. So after exchanging the table, I drove back home to Pembroke. When I arrived at my apartment, I installed my table, stood back, and laughed. My new table matched perfectly with the framed purple irises that I had recently hung on my wall.

A few weeks earlier, I had had some water damage in my closet. It was there that I kept the large water jugs that I had brought from a source in Fort-Coulonge. When I was done cleaning up the mess, I felt that there was something in my boxes that must have wanted to come out. So I opened all of the boxes to check what was inside. I found two picture frames and a painting of my favorite flower, purple irises. I had not yet taken the time to really decorate, so I decided to hang them on the wall. Now, on arriving home with my great find, I found that my new Reiki table brought out the magnificent color purple of the irises in my frames. I realized that angels are much better at decorating than I am. I was glad I listened to them.

You also have access to this divine guidance. Follow your inspiration and intuition, let yourself be guided by the angels, and do not doubt their ability to help you decorate your life and your home.

Dressing Up with the Angels

I am not one of those "organized" people who prepares her clothes for the next day. I never know how I am going to feel when I wake up, so I let the angels guide me in the morning. I take my shower and ask, "What should I wear today?" There is always an image that comes to mind of an ensemble that I should wear or a feeling for a certain outfit in which I would be comfortable. As I have said, I am a very clairsentient person, so I love the textures of clothing. When I look at old pictures of my youth, I cannot always remember what was happening when the photo was taken, but I remember the texture of the clothes I was wearing. I remember how I felt in the clothes and how the material felt to the touch. That may be why I wanted to be a clothes designer when I was young.

If you listen to your divine guidance, you will always feel good in your clothes and they will look great on you. You will always wear the perfect color for you that day. When I need energy, I am attracted to yellow or brighter colors. I notice that when I wear pink, I feel soft and sweet. The angels always suggest that I wear white for my conferences and workshops.

Do not hesitate to ask the angels for advice before getting dressed in the morning. You will not only look amazing but feel amazing too!

Shopping with the Angels

I always go shopping with my angels. Whether it is at the grocery store or a clothing store, I invite them to join me. As I pull up to the mall, I start by asking for a space near the door. I drive as close to the entrance as possible, and most of the time I will find an empty space or notice a car about to leave. Before going into the store, I set my intention: "Let's make this quick, easy, and on sale." I enter the store, find what I am looking for, usually on sale or at a good price, and leave.

For example, one day I was shopping for a new top for my book launch that same evening. It was lunchtime and I didn't have much time. So I entered a boutique at the mall and asked the angels to help me find the perfect top quickly and on sale. I noticed it as soon as I walked in. It was beautiful and perfect. It was a very feminine white linen top with flowing and graceful sleeves, plus it was on sale! It didn't take me more than fifteen minutes to go in and get out with my great buy.

When you are shopping with your angels, say to them, "Thank you, my angels, for helping me find the perfect _____ for me."

Renovating with the Angels

I invite the angels to help me with all my projects, both personal and at work. When I found a house at the beach with the help of the angels, it needed some TLC. They gave me the idea to make a downstairs apartment to help pay the mortgage. One day while I was at the gym, I talked to the owner about my project. I knew she and her husband bought homes and flipped them, so I inquired about where she bought her cabinets. She asked, "You're looking for kitchen cabinets?"

"Yes," I answered.

She told me that she actually had some cabinets in her garage that she had purchased for a project but that they had changed their mind. So I drove by her house after work to see the cabinets and they were absolutely perfect for an apartment. She informed me that her carpenter was even available to install them, as they were between projects. So he came to my house and installed the cabinets in the basement apartment. He told me, "You must have been born under a lucky star because the cabinets fit just right in the opening in the wall." It was so true! The cabinets were a perfect fit between two walls and there wasn't an inch too much or too little.

The angels found me an almost new fridge and stove for an excellent price. My painter was available, and even my tiler, who supposedly needed to be booked at least three months in advance, was available for my renovations. Was that just luck? I don't think so.

I believe that there is a perfection in my life because I don't try to control everything. Admittedly, I am not perfect. Sometimes I get the urge to control and feel impatient, but I remind myself to trust. I ask my angels to help me, I listen to and follow their guidance, and I trust. And when things do not go as I would like, I tell myself that it is just not the right time. I stop and wait. We must not rush, push, or try to control, as this only slows our progress.

We must be patient and trust that everything will happen at the right time. Everything is always perfect. We don't always see why things are not progressing as we would like, but we have to trust that everything will work for our highest good. There is a divine plan for us, and we usually are not aware of everything that this implies, but God and the angels know. They want only what is best for us, so we must learn to trust.

Managing Our Schedule with the Angels

Angels can even help us manage our time. A very good friend of mine was supposed to visit me one weekend, but I did not feel that I had the energy to properly receive her. Not wanting to offend her, I asked my angels for help. The very next day, my friend called to tell me she would not be able to visit because of a change in her schedule. I was so relieved. We rescheduled the visit for another weekend that turned out to be much better for us both.

You can also ask your angels to help you with your time management and energy. Always ask that things work out for the greatest good of all.

I believe that angels are always directing our path, like when I was shopping for a house at the beach. That week, I visited two houses. On Monday I visited a home for sale by the owner, and on Tuesday I toured one being sold by a real estate agent. I had spent most of the week researching the house that was for sale by the owner. The following week, I was supposed to go on a business trip. The Sunday before my departure, I checked the weather and they were announcing a blizzard that was going to last for three days on the Lower North Shore of Quebec. So I decided to postpone my trip because I did not want to spend the week waiting in airports. On Monday morning, as I pulled into the parking lot at the office, I had a very strong feeling, almost a sense of urgency, that the house I had visited with the agent was for me.

So I called the agent and made an appointment to revisit the house that same day. I believed the angels really wanted me to have that house. If there hadn't been a blizzard, I would have been away on business all week and maybe the house would have been sold while I was gone. Or maybe if I had made an offer a week later, the people who did my renovations might not have been so available. Do you see the perfection in our lives? You just need to look for it or ask the angels to show it to you.

A change of plans can happen to any of us, but it is up to us how we choose to respond to these changes. To me, life is like going down a river in a canoe. We don't always know all the contingencies that may arise, but we can still go with the flow. It is much less tiring to go with the flow than to fight the current. Always look for a positive reason why certain things occur and certain things do not. There is always a good reason for everything. You just have to find it or ask your angels to help you see it. Stay open to all changes. Know that changes are really only opportunities. It is up to you to discover what opportunities are being presented to you.

Health with the Angels

The angels can even help us manage or improve our health. We can ask our angels to help us relieve our pain or even help us understand our symptoms. For example, at one point I was experiencing symptoms such as headaches and cramps, and I asked my angels to tell me what I needed to do to reduce the symptoms. I distinctly heard the word "magnesium," and when I searched for it on the Internet, I found that I had several symptoms of magnesium deficiency.

My grandmother Josephine told me before her passing that one day she had asked to know what was happening with her eyesight, which had deteriorated significantly in a short time. She then clearly heard the words "face blind." Prosopagnosia is the inability to recognize familiar faces. She told me that she had heard the words as if someone had whispered them in her ear. She asked us to research the topic and we discovered that this condition can be the result of an accidental trauma. My grandmother had fallen down the stairs and had developed prosopagnosia soon after.

Do not hesitate to ask your angels for guidance regarding your own health. Stay open to what you see on television, topics being discussed around you, or even "words" that are whispered in your ear. Angels will find a way to communicate to you exactly what you need.

Manifesting a House with the Angels

Manifesting a house or an apartment is a great opportunity to commune with the angels. Take the time to tell the angels what you deeply desire in your new home and the reasons why. Your home is a reflection of who you are, so it is important that it reflect you well. Take time to really think about what you want. Even if you are in a hurry because you are moving to another city for work, you have time to commune with the angels and ask them to go ahead of you to find your perfect home. Trust them. They will be delighted that you even asked.

The angels say that to manifest a house or an apartment, first you have to believe that what you want exists. You must also feel worthy of receiving it, stay open to all of the possibilities that may arrive, imagine in your mind what you would like, and be grateful to the angels in advance for answering your prayers.

Next, you need to take *guided* action. Don't force anything. Tell your friends exactly what you are looking for, call a real estate agent, and also drive around the neighborhoods in which you wish to live. Look for signs that might tell you that this is the house for you. Stay open to all of the possibilities, meaning go visit a home that might be priced higher than what you are willing to pay. Maybe the seller is ready to lower the price. Do not limit yourself. Remember that a miracle is about to happen. God and the angels have a perfect home just for you. Do not be discouraged and do not lose faith. Sometimes it can take a little time, but tell yourself that perhaps the seller has not yet listed your house. There is always a good reason for everything. Stay confident that the angels are working hard to bring you what you want. Thank them every day for finding you your perfect home.

I have manifested two houses in my life. The first was in 2007 when I had just left my boyfriend. I had searched for an apartment but had found nothing to my liking. I wanted something special, not an ordinary apartment.

One morning I woke up with a strong desire to buy a house. I went to work, and around 1:00 pm I met up with my supervisor. He asked me how things were going and I told him, "I decided I want to buy a house!" He told me that his wife, who just happened to be a real estate agent, had just viewed a new home for sale that morning and he thought that it would be the perfect house for me. So I said to him, "It must be mine! God and the angels always answer my prayers pretty quickly!"

I called his wife and made an appointment for 4:30 pm. Later that day we toured the house, which was a cute little home on a corner lot. The neighbors weren't too close, so there was privacy as well as a view of the ocean. I noticed that the house would require a little love to be to my liking.

I visited a second house that evening near the beach. It has always been a dream of mine to live near the beach. The view from this house was amazing! The house was smaller than the first one and was built *on* the beach. However, I did have concerns. I wondered if water in the basement had ever been a problem. It seemed likely, given the location and the fact that the house had been built so low. It was a steep drive up to the street. Another concern was that of driving up to the main road in the wintertime; the snow accumulation could be terrible, which would make accessing the road difficult.

My mother and I went out for dinner that evening, and after some discussion I called the real estate agent to make an offer on the corner-lot house. In my agent's office that night, I noticed a heart-shaped stone in a jar on her desk. I knew it had to be a sign because I see hearts everywhere. She had never noticed it before and graciously offered it to me.

The next day, everything was negotiated. It all happened so quickly and easily. This was at a time when there were very few houses on the market, but I had faith that God and the angels would bring me the perfect home. I had no doubt that they wanted what was in my highest good. Everything is possible with faith.

Selling a House with the Angels

Sometimes it may seem difficult to sell a house. I know a lady that had a house on the market for a couple of years and there were no offers. The house was rented, so it wasn't urgent to sell. When she talked to me about it, I sensed that she was still very attached to the house and I explained to her that I felt that she wasn't ready to let it go. So we did an exercise to cut the cords from the bottoms of her feet, because that is where we attach ourselves to a house or location.

I asked the lady to sit down on a chair and hold her feet out one at a time. I asked the Archangel Michael to come with his sword and help me cut the cords that were linking her feet to the house. I made a firm cut with my right hand about six inches from the bottom of her feet and asked her to say out loud, "I am willing to cut the cords to the house." Less than a month later, she received an offer and the house was sold.

When I put my second house up for sale, I received a few visits the first week and then nothing. I knew something had to be preventing the house from selling. Then I received a phone call and I noticed my heart drop and the thought "Oh no, it's someone for the house!" That's when I realized that I was preventing the sale, because I was attached to it. So I walked into the house, into every room, and thanked it for all it had given me. I told it how grateful I was for the wonderful moments and all the love. I told it I had to go because God and the angels were calling me elsewhere. Next, I said a prayer: "Dear God and my loving angels, please bring me someone that will love and honor this house as much as I did. Please make the sale quick and easy and for a reasonable price. Thank you, thank you, thank you."

The next day I received a call. When I opened the door to welcome the potential buyers, I knew in my heart that the house was meant for them. They made me a reasonable offer without any conditions. It was a quick and easy sale, just as I had requested.

Prayer for Manifesting a House or an Apartment

Here is a sample prayer that you can use to help manifest your dream home or apartment.

Worthiness

"Lord God, I am worthy of your goodness, your grace, and your blessings. By the simple fact that I exist, I am worthy of a beautiful home. I free myself from all negative emotions and false beliefs that I have about my worthiness. I am confident that the perfect house for me exists and is waiting for me. I know that even if the market is high, a perfect home for me exists that I am able to afford. I believe that even if the market is stagnant, there is a perfect buyer for my house who is willing to pay a fair price. I know that my will is your will and you only want what is best for me."

Desire

"Dearest angels, I desire a beautiful home in which I will be well and that I can afford, with a lovely view and quiet neighbors."

Trust

"My dearest angels, I trust you completely. I know you have heard my request and are already working on its fulfillment. I remain open to all possibilities that are presented to me. I promise you, my dearest angels, to follow your divine guidance."

Imagination

I reserve at least ten minutes a day to imagine the house or apartment of my dreams. I imagine myself already living there. I feel the joy of living in my dream home.

Gratitude

"Thank you in advance, Lord God and my dearest angels, for the fulfillment of my greatest desire, to have a great home in which I will be well and that I can afford, with a lovely view and quiet neighbors. I am grateful that you have always found the most beautiful and perfect places for me to live in the past and I thank you now. Thank you, thank you, thank you."

EXERCISE
Life with the Angels

Invite the angels into your everyday life to help you. From the moment you wake up in the morning, thank your loving angels for being with you and invite them to guide all of your choices. Ask for their help with your morning routine, choosing the right clothes for the day, having a safe drive to and from work, and assisting you with all of your projects, whether they are related to work or home.

Bring your angels shopping with you and work with them to redecorate your home. Ask them for guidance regarding your health, career, and finances, and even your love life.

Sit with them every morning and listen to their guidance. Follow your heart when you are shopping and listen for the tiny nudging when you go about your day.

Say to them, "Thank you, my darling angels, for finding me the perfect _____!"

Manifesting a House or an Apartment

Whether you are relocating to a new area or simply moving across town, your angels can help you manifest your perfect new home. Here are a few simple steps to get you on your way to manifesting your next dream home or apartment.

Worthiness

Write down your current beliefs about house hunting or selling, such as the following:

+ "The market is not good for selling a house right now."
+ "I will never find a home that suits my needs."
+ "The market is too high for me to be able to purchase a house."

For each of your beliefs, ask yourself if this belief is serving to attract a new home to you or repel it.

For each of your beliefs, write down what you are ready to release:

+ "I release the belief that the market is not good for selling a house right now."
+ "I release the belief that I will never find a home that suits me."
+ "I release the belief that the market is too high for me to purchase a house."

Now create new beliefs:

- "The perfect home or apartment for me exists and is waiting for me."
- "Even if the market is high, I know there is a perfect home for me that I am able to afford."
- "Even if the market is stagnant, I know there is a perfect buyer for my house who is willing to pay a fair price."

Desire

Ask yourself, "What do I really desire in a house or an apartment to be happy? What do I truly need?"

Then answer: "I desire a beautiful home in which I will be well and that I can afford. I would like this new home to have a lovely view and quiet neighbors."

Trust

Take guided action. Drive around the neighborhood in which you wish to live and look for signs that might tell you that this is the house for you. Call a real estate agent and your friends and tell them what you are looking for in a home. Stay open to all of the possibilities. Go visit a home that is priced higher than what you are willing to pay. Maybe the seller is ready to lower the price. Do not limit yourself. Remember that a miracle is about to happen. God and the angels have a perfect home just for you. Do not be discouraged and do not lose faith. Sometimes it can take a little time, but tell yourself that perhaps the seller has not yet listed your house. There is always a good reason for everything. Stay confident that the angels are working hard to bring you what you want.

Imagination

Imagine exactly what you would like in a new home. Imagine especially how you want to feel in your new home. How much space do you need? Do you want trees, a backyard, a pool, or a spa? How do you imagine the kitchen, the living room, and the other rooms?

To help you with your research, you can ask your angels to show you an image or picture of your new neighborhood.

Describe your ideal home.

Gratitude

Write down everything for which you are grateful at this present moment, such as "I am grateful that you have always found me beautiful homes in the past that were absolutely perfect for me."

9
MANIFESTING HEALTH

"When someone desires health,
we must first ask him if he is ready to remove
the cause of his illness. Only then can you help."
—*Hippocrates*

Disease is the language of the soul. Our soul uses disease to communicate that which is often unconscious. If we are listening, the disease can tell us a lot about how we feel and how we perceive life.

Our present health care system would have us believe that we are victims of our diseases, but in fact it is we who create them. There is still a lot of resistance to this way of seeing disease, but there is also growing scientific evidence that proves that the cells of our body are affected by our subconscious thoughts and beliefs, as described in the book *Biology of Belief* by Bruce Lipton, renowned American biologist. In fact, the only thing that is inherited is how we react to life. We adopt beliefs and imitate ways of reacting to things from our parents and they from their parents, and it is because of our perception of life that we develop disease. According to Dr. Lipton, all of this happens on the subconscious level.

There are different reasons for which we can develop a disease. Disease can help us become conscious of the fact that we are no longer happy in a certain situation. We may have a soul contract with another person to live the experience of a disease. We may also use a disease as a form of procrastination. While we are caring for our illness, we may not be fulfilling our life's purpose. Sometimes the disease can be a form of self-punishment. If you feel guilty, you can hurt yourself by having an "accident." We may also use a disease to punish the people around us and guilt them into caring for us. We may use an illness to attract love and attention from our loved ones. If you need a break from your life but feel unable to take time off out of fear of displeasing someone, you can attract an accident where you break something in order to break out of the routine of your life. You may also create a depression or an occupational burnout. That is one way your soul signals to you that you have temporarily lost your joy of living, you are not aligned with what your soul really wants you to do, or you are not setting proper limits and boundaries.

Before looking at how we may try to cure a disease or ease discomfort, we must first understand what it is trying to tell us. And we cannot speak of healing without discussing prevention.

Prevention

If the cells in our body are affected by our subconscious thoughts and beliefs, then we can conclude that to prevent disease we must first be aware of our beliefs, our thoughts, our perceptions, and our reactions to certain life circumstances and how we express these in our lives.

Thoughts create. If we repeat a negative or positive thought long enough, the thoughts will eventually materialize. For example, repeating "I can, I can, I can ... !" will ensure that you can. Repeating the words "I can't!" often enough will ensure that you won't.

Here is an example of how thoughts create. In 2003, I went to Toronto for a healing Mass. There was a Catholic nun there who had the gift of healing. There were several thousand people in the room that day. Toward the end of the Mass, the nun walked through the aisles with a relic. When she passed by me, I felt something change in my body. I had been suffering from ulcerative colitis for over a year by that time. Over the next few days, I did not bleed. Every time I went to the bathroom, I thought, "It's unbelievable!" On the fourth day, I started to bleed again. What I realized was that my thoughts were creating my reality. I had kept repeating the words "It's unbelievable," which actually meant that I could not believe, and so I undid the miracle. Today, I simple say "Thank you" and "That's amazing."

Thoughts create, and words spoken with strong emotions create even faster.

The angels suggest we remain aware of what we are thinking and saying. Let's look at how some common expressions may affect our body and even cause disease. For example, how do you think these expressions will affect your body?

+ "I just can't digest what he said or did!"
+ "It burns me!"
+ "It's killing me!"
+ "It tore me apart!"

When these words are used with strong emotions, it can register in the body and develop into indigestion or heartburn or even cause disease in the stomach or colon.

Here are some examples of how common expressions can affect the body:

Expressions	Area Affected
"I'm in a pinch!"	Sciatic nerve
"It breaks my heart!"	Heart
"I feel torn!"	Tear in the rectum
"It pisses me off!"	Bladder

Do you recognize any expressions you use in your own life?

Do you have any discomfort or illness now? What expressions are you using that may be related to your disease?

To stay conscious of your thoughts and expressions, make a pact with those around you or ask your angels to help you notice when you use negative words that can harm your health. Say, "Thank you, my dearest angels, for helping me stay aware of any expressions I have been using that may be negatively affecting my health."

If you feel a strong desire to express your frustration, be aware of how your perception of the situation may be hurting you and your body. Anger is always self-directed. When we are angry at someone, we are usually angry at ourselves for putting ourselves in the situation, for not speaking up or setting healthy boundaries, for letting ourselves be taken advantage of, and especially for not loving and respecting ourselves enough. Most of the time we do these things out of a fear of not being loved for who we really are.

Fear is the biggest cause of disease. In fact, there are only two true emotions: love and fear. Anything that is not love is fear. Anger is simply fear disguised. Resentment, sadness, and feelings of disempowerment and stress are all simply fear disguised. We are afraid of not being loved, of not being lovable, of not being good enough. We then attract people and situations that confirm this belief, and this keeps us in a state of fear and stress.

At times, you might be dealing with a person or situation that makes you so angry, so irritated, and so resentful, even to the point of feeling "beside yourself," that you feel the need to express your feelings. Yes, you must express them. You must expel the anger and all negative emotions from your body. So take your pillow and show it who's boss. Go for a run or take a boxing class. Get your anger out and then see how you can express your needs to the person in a calm and loving manner. Ask the Archangels Michael and Raphael to help you find the right words to express yourself in a loving and calm way and for the greatest good of all. Prepare your speech well, and talk about the facts and how your needs and expectations have not been met. It is best to let some time pass between the incident and the moment when you express yourself so as to do it in a calm and loving manner. When we are full of strong emotions such as anger and frustration, the most important thing is to change our perception. Try to see the other person's point of view and try to let go of any negative emotions that may be keeping you in a state of disease and discomfort.

Ask Archangel Michael to help you guard your thoughts and to ensure that they are loving toward yourself as well as others. Archangel Gabriel is wonderful at helping you communicate your feelings better, and Archangel Raphael can help you heal your relationships. Ask the archangels to help you speak your truth, be true to yourself, and set healthy boundaries. Archangel Uriel can help you shed light on any situation. If you find yourself in a situation or relationship that is ambiguous or unhealthy, ask Archangel Uriel to help you see the situation clearly.

You can say, "Thank you, dearest archangels, for helping me see this situation more clearly. Help me be true to myself and to my needs. Thank you for the strength and confidence to speak my truth and set healthy boundaries. Help me find the courage and the right words to express myself in a loving and firm manner. Help us heal this relationship for the greatest good of all. Thank you, thank you, thank you."

On a final note regarding how our words create, the angels suggest we refrain from discussing our disease in too much detail. Whenever you talk about your disease, you anchor it more firmly in your body. Aside from the weather, disease is the most discussed topic in our society. Listen to the people around you in the coffee shops or elsewhere; they mostly talk about how bad they feel. Choose to discuss your symptoms only with your doctor. When someone asks you "How are you?" simply answer, "I'm well and so happy to see you!" Focus your attention on positive topics and events.

Disease

Disease or illness is always an invitation to reconnect with our true selves. When we become ill or develop a disease, it is a sign that we have temporarily lost touch with our higher self. The word *disease* means "we are not at ease," meaning we are not at peace within our lives.

The angels say that it is not only important but vital to be true to ourselves. I know it is not always easy to do this, because we were raised to please others. We want to please our spouse, our parents, our family, our friends, and our employers at all costs. Many of us would rather hurt ourselves before hurting someone else. We let ourselves down rather than let someone else down. We also forget ourselves in day-to-day life. We put the needs of others before our own. Our own deepest desires remain buried deep inside our hearts, and with time, we forget about them and sometimes blame the people around us because we did not realize our dreams.

When we become sick or exhausted, our deepest desires will try to surface. If you're listening and you take the time to care for yourself, to recover and rest, your soul will try to communicate to you your most heartfelt longings. The angels suggest you take time out of your life to go inside and listen and gain perspective, whether it is through a daily mediation, a weekend retreat, or a month away from your life, like they suggested to me. When we take time to connect with our angels and our inner self, we make space for their loving messages and guidance to be heard.

Ever since our incarnation, our body has been recording everything that has happened emotionally. When you develop symptoms, stop and ask yourself, "What is going on in my life?" Have you ever noticed that there is almost always a significant event that happened right before the symptoms first appeared? When we are unable to express ourselves or manage a stressful situation, our body, which is really our ally, our greatest friend, tries to manage this stress for us.

Whenever you deny yourself, a cell in your body dies. Whenever you give your power away to another person, such as an employer or a partner, whenever you put yourself down or feel disempowered about a situation, a part of you dies. When we listen to and follow what our heart truly desires, when we are able to set limits and boundaries and truly honor our feelings and needs and are loving and respecting ourselves, we feel at peace and experience wellness.

Wellness, or well-being, is the opposite of disease. When we are being our true selves, when we are well with ourselves and others, we are totally at peace and can be disease-free.

Deep down, a lot of us know this, but it doesn't prevent us from experiencing disease. I can relate. I have experienced my own share of disease, including an appendicitis, acute ulcerative colitis for twelve years, eczema, and shingles. Through all of these diseases, I tried to understand what my body was trying to tell me, what my soul really wanted me to know. Once I understood that feelings of worry, fear, and stress were at the root of these diseases, I took action to change the situation and my perception of it. Now I try to stay in a state of calmness and peacefulness through meditation and by relinquishing all my worries and problems to God and the angels.

For example, before going to bed, I say, "Thank you, God and my dearest angels, for caring for _____ (current problem or worry). I know you already have all the solutions. Thank you for bringing me creative ideas to resolve this issue and for helping me feel at peace."

Often I will wake up feeling peaceful and have an ingenious idea about how to solve my problem or ease my worries.

Disease in Children

Some of you may ask, "But how do you explain diseases in children and newborns?" The angels tell me that newborn children sometimes arrive with diseases they had in their previous life, such as a child being born with cataracts. A fetus may also be affected by a stressful event that happened during the pregnancy. Children may also develop disease in early childhood when they experience stress in the home or at school. It is important not to blame anyone or feel guilty, but simply to be aware of the symptoms and see how you can change the atmosphere in your home, help the child adapt at school, or learn to express themselves.

Some souls choose to come into this world to live the experience of a disease to learn something or to teach others. Sick children are often our greatest teachers. If you take the time to listen to them, you will see that they are much wiser than you think. I have often heard parents of seriously ill children or children who have passed away at a young age report that their child taught them a lot about life and that they were a real gift from heaven.

Remember that there is always a reason for everything. Every experience brings a lesson and nothing happens for nothing. Wanting to blame someone or feeling guilty does not elevate our consciousness. It is best to look at any situation and try to understand what lessons can be learned and what blessings you are being offered. Ask your angels, "Dearest angels, please help me understand the gifts and blessings in this disease."

The Language of Disease

Our body speaks to us through ailments and disease. How can we understand what it is trying to tell us? The angels tell me that "the consequence of our discomfort or illness is the cause."

There are three important questions to ask yourself:

1. How do I feel physically? Irritated, inflamed, tight, stuck, stiff, etc.?
2. How do I feel emotionally about my discomfort? Anxious, panicked, paralyzed, disappointed, scared, nervous, sad, etc.?
3. Do I feel the same way in another area of my life? Like in my family, friendships, work, finances, love life, etc.?

Take a good look at your life and see if the words you use to describe your emotional and physical discomfort also describe another area of your life. The words are always clues to the real issues in your life.

Next, thank your body for the message: "Thank you, body (name the specific part), for your message and for your love and support. I know that you are my best friend and you are showing me what I need to know."

Once you have zeroed in on the situation that is causing your discomfort, you can look at how you can resolve it.

You can make an action plan to reduce your stress, face your fears, express your needs, forgive others, forgive yourself, and do what you need to do to be at peace.

Here is an example:

You have very sore legs that are preventing you from walking easily.

How do you feel physically? "I have trouble moving forward. I lack flexibility and feel stiff."

How do you feel emotionally about your discomfort? "I feel angry. I'm scared and worried."

Do you feel the same way in another area of your life? Take a look at your life to see if you are having trouble moving forward in a project, a relationship, or at work. Do you lack flexibility to move forward with something or someone? Are you afraid to move forward in your life? Is your fear of moving forward irritating you, making you scared and worried, and ultimately preventing you from experiencing joy?

Take a look at your life and try to understand what your body is telling you. Talk with your body, thank it for the message, and take action to correct the situation.

Tell your body, "Thank you for the message! I understand now. I will get into action to move forward in my life! Despite the fear, I will take small guided steps forward!"

If you have any difficulty with this exercise, ask Archangel Raphael to help you understand what you need to know: "Thank you, Archangel Raphael, for helping find the right words to describe my pain and discomfort and for helping see which part of my life I need to heal in order to help heal my body. I know my body is my friend and is lovingly holding on to this pain to help me see it better in my own life. I am willing to look honestly at any situation or relationship that may be affecting my health, and I am willing to let go of any fear, worry, beliefs, or resentment that may be preventing me from experiencing perfect health. Thank you, thank you, thank you."

One of my clients had really bad low back pain. It was so serious that she had to remain in bed for a month so as not to put any pressure on her spine. Pain in the lower back is usually associated with the fear of lacking money, so I asked her the following questions:

How do you feel physically? "I feel paralyzed. I feel pressure in my lower back and I also feel as if the nerves are pinched."

How do you feel emotionally about your discomfort? " I feel angry and irritated, and at the same time I'm scared and worried."

Do you feel the same way in another area of your life? This lady wanted to build a new home but was afraid of not having enough money. She was literally paralyzed by her fear and concern about money. She had to delay the project because of her back pain. She was putting a lot of pressure on herself and felt pinched financially.

Today, she is fine. She relieved some of the pressure by choosing a new house plan with which she felt much more comfortable financially. She secured a great mortgage rate that allowed her to pay off the house more quickly than expected. She no longer feels stuck. She is no longer afraid of not having enough money because she made the right decisions to remove the financial pressure.

I also had a personal healing experience by being aware of my symptoms. One morning I arrived in the office parking lot, when suddenly I felt something in my back that felt like an electric shock. I immediately asked my angels what it was, and the answer that came to me was one word: "shingles." My mother and grandmother had both experienced this disease. I knew that shingles was very painful and could last for several months.

When I arrived at my office, I researched the symptoms on the Internet and soon discovered that the sensation of an electric shock was indeed a symptom of shingles.

At the end of the day, I was in such pain that I had a difficult time picking up groceries. I asked myself the following questions:

How do you feel physically? "I felt a shock this morning and now I feel intense pain and stiffness. I feel like something has a grip on my back."

How do you feel emotionally about your discomfort? "I feel very anxious because I certainly do not want to have this pain for months. I feel very afraid, nervous, and sad."

Do you feel similarly in another area of your life? "In my relationship, I feel trapped. I experienced a shocking situation with my boyfriend recently. I do not want to endure this painful relationship and his rigidity (stiffness) for several more months. I feel anxious and nervous. I am afraid to tell him about my decision to leave and I am also sad that our relationship is not working out."

I also read the following sentences in Jacques Martel's book *The Complete Dictionary of Ailments and Diseases*: "I felt under attack ... A situation or person has hurt me, provoking tension ... The pain reminds me of a forced submission to some authority ... I feel in constant danger ... I hold back my creative energies ... I am feeling an intense emotional reaction or irritation over someone or something that causes me excessive stress and makes my decision-making difficult."

This was exactly what I was experiencing. I was going through a very difficult period with my boyfriend and I knew I had to leave. He tried to convince me to stay, and I felt torn. I loved him but could no longer live with him. I felt I couldn't be myself. I had dreams to fulfill, and for me, those dreams were vital. I was to the point where I preferred to die rather than not fulfill God's will.

Being in so much pain that evening, I ran a bath, hoping it would calm my nerves. I used a salt ball that my mother had given me some time before. When the ball was completely melted, a piece of plastic remained in my hand, on which it was written, "We must accept a man for who he is and not for who we wish he was."

What a revelation! It was clear that my image of my boyfriend was not who he really was … and I could not accept him as he was. He had some great qualities, but I felt I could no longer grow with him. Our story was over.

So I prayed to my angels that night and told them that if I woke up the next morning with no symptoms, I was going to love myself enough to get out of the relationship. That evening, two of my friends confirmed that they would help me the next day. I knew they were sent to me by the angels to help me through that difficult time in my life. They were real earth angels who took time out of their busy lives to help me move. The next morning I woke up without any pain, and I kept the promise I had made to the angels.

There are a few excellent books that exist on the subject of the link between physical symptoms and emotional blockages, including *You Can Heal Your Life* and *Heal Your Body* by Louise L. Hay and *The Complete Dictionary of Ailments and Diseases* by Jacques Martel.

Healing

Healing has always been an important part of my private consultations. We all have emotional healing to do. It is an ongoing process. In 2004, during one of my earliest readings, the angels recommended that we start healing our lives by reviewing the major events that have happened over the years so that it becomes easier to heal our daily issues. They invite us to forgive ourselves as well as others. We have all done things in our lives that we are not proud of, and we have all experienced incidents with our parents, families, friends, lovers, and even strangers that have affected us. We have all lived through painful experiences during our childhood. We must take the time to address this emotional baggage. We must forgive ourselves and everyone else for everything. In fact, life is forgiving. Life is about giving love and compassion to ourselves and others. Jesus's main commandment was "Love one another."

Self-Forgiveness

The angels suggest we start by forgiving ourselves first. If we take a good look at our own behavior and forgive ourselves, we will be more forgiving toward others. When we see something in another person that we don't like, it is usually a sign that it is something we do not like and accept about ourselves. Accepting and loving ourselves for who we are enables us to love and accept others as they are.

Make a list of all the people you have hurt, and describe your regrets. Go over this list with compassion and love for yourself, remembering that you are a soul trying to find your way home. You are a beautiful spiritual being living a human experience. Sometimes we have to experience who we are *not* to decide who we really want to be.

It can be very healing to call or talk with the person you have hurt and apologize for your trespasses. Letting the other person know that you are aware of your wrongs is a beautiful lesson in humility. Whether or not the person chooses to forgive you is not important. What is important is that you forgive yourself. You cannot change how other people choose to feel or react. You can only choose your own actions. You can choose to love yourself, to be and to do better. Forgiving yourself is the greatest act of self-love.

Make a list of everything you have done or think you did for which you may need to forgive yourself. Ask Archangel Raphael to accompany you during this exercise, and use a green pen or pencil. The beautiful and loving healing energy of Archangel Raphael is emerald green. He says that when we write with green ink, everything we write is instantly healed.

Is there anything on your list that is really so unforgivable? Is there anything that you would not forgive someone else? Give yourself the same forgiveness that you would give to others.

For each thing on your list, look in the mirror and say this sentence out loud: "I forgive myself for _____. I did my best with the knowledge I had at that time."

Forgiveness of Others

Forgiving others is essential for our well-being. We do not extend forgiveness to others for them, but mostly for ourselves. Often the other person continues to go on with life and does not even think about their transgressions. The person may not even be aware of their actions. But you continue to hurt yourself by keeping all the anger, shame, and guilt inside of you.

We all hang on to feelings of blame, anger, frustration, resentment, hatred, anxiety, fear, disappointment guilt, shame, insecurity, and depression. Know that these feelings contribute to our discomfort and diseases. When we feel anything but love, peace, and joy, it is a sign that we are not aligned with *who we really are*, and a disease can develop.

The angels recommend that we sit quietly and ask Archangel Gabriel (the angel of communication) and Archangel Raphael (the angel of healing) to assist us with our healing process.

The archangels suggest that we get a notebook or journal and use a green pen to write our story. Archangel Raphael says to use a green pen to help with the healing of anything we put on paper.

First, we can begin to write our story from the time we were children up until now. We can write about all the main events we experienced and of all the negative feelings we felt regarding the events. Expressing these feelings is vital to our well-being. We must be totally honest about our feelings, about the actions of other people and any beliefs we may have developed as a result.

Once our story is written, the angels suggest we go through each event and find the lesson, the gift, that this person or event brought us.

If there is a particular person you need to forgive, you can ask yourself the following questions:

What do I need to forgive the person for?

How did I feel during this event?

How has this event affected the rest of my life?

What beliefs have I developed as a result of this event?

What have I learned from this situation?

What good has this event brought me?

What qualities did I develop after this event?

What is the gift of this transgression?

Answer each question and finish with a sentence of forgiveness, such as "I understand that you could not have done any better with the knowledge and life experience you had at the time. With the help of my angels, I accept that this event happened and I forgive you. I free myself from all negative emotions related to this event."

It is not necessary to send anything to anyone. The goal is to release any negative emotions and forgive.

The angels want you to remember that you chose to come to this earth to experience certain specific events that helped you become the person you are today. Without these experiences, you could not accomplish your life's purpose. You have soul contracts with the people who are in your life: the ones who have hurt you in the past or who are hurting you now or may hurt you in the future. These people have chosen to live this drama with you to teach you *the* very thing your soul needs to learn so it can continue to evolve. This is a fundamental truth about our existence.

I know that for some people this truth may be hard to accept. But know that the people who hurt you the most are the *souls* who love you the most. They are your greatest teachers. These souls experience the greatest test because to hurt someone goes against the purity and perfection of our true self. In fact, these souls have sacrificed themselves to come to earth with you and teach you the lessons of forgiveness, acceptance, hope, courage, confidence, joy, and love. So see these souls as the beautiful and magnificent beings they really are and have compassion for them. Send them love and thank them for agreeing to fulfill this role in your life, for without them, you could not fulfill your soul contract and your divine life's purpose. I find it helps to look at them and imagine the pain they must be experiencing deep inside that makes them behave in a certain way. Imagine how painful it must be to lack self-confidence and self-esteem, to not feel loved or lovable to the point of hurting others. Try to sense their pain and feel compassion for them.

For some of you, what happened to you may be so painful and atrocious that you have difficulty feeling love or compassion for the other person. The angels suggest you at least try to accept that the event occurred and try to see how the event may have positively affected your life. See how maybe it made you stronger, more courageous, more determined and resilient, or even set you on a specific path toward something more wonderful. There is always something positive in every situation and there is always a reason for everything; we must simply look to find it. No experience is wasted with God. Everything happens for us and not to us. And real healing starts with acceptance.

Institutions

On a larger scale, many of us have resentment toward our institutions, governments, and various cultural societies. The angels have helped me understand, accept, and forgive the injustices in the world, reminding me that I have done my part to create them. As in our current life, where we are creating all that is before us, we have also created the past in our former lives.

We created this world in which we live, including all that we love and hate about it. As creators, we have to love and accept our creation. We have to accept responsibility for what exists in the world, and acceptance is the first step toward healing. Acceptance does not mean we have to live with things the way they are; it only means that we should drop the negative feelings we have toward the situation and strive to change it. It does not serve us to complain about any system if we do not intend to contribute to effecting change.

At any time, we can choose to create a better life for ourselves and a better world for us all. We can do this with healing and forgiveness, by accepting and loving everything that we have created and choosing to create again with a new consciousness.

Conclusion on Healing

The angels gave me all this advice about healing during a private reading in 2004. At that time, I did the exercises for self-forgiveness and the forgiveness of others, which are presented at the end of this chapter. I even called some people I felt I had hurt to tell them that I was aware of their pain and wanted them to know. I told them it was not necessary for them to forgive me because it was me who had to forgive myself. One of these people has since become one of my best friends.

After writing this book and before its publication in French, I was going through a difficult period. I felt a deep sadness. I felt that something was blocking me and was not allowing me to move easily forward in the direction of my dreams. I am humble enough to admit that even with all these tools that the angels have offered me over the previous ten years, I could not do it alone. Through a friend, the angels led me to a healing center, where I discovered that I had wounds buried so deep that I had completely forgotten they were there. You cannot heal what you do not acknowledge or remember. Once I became aware of these old wounds and I did the forgiveness exercises, I finally felt free. It was like everything that was blocking me, that was preventing me from living my life fully and being all that God intended me to be, was transformed.

That therapy session was the most beautiful experience of my life! There is no greater voyage than the one we make inside of ourselves. I thank my angels and my friend who guided me toward the center and for the wonderful therapy I experienced.

If you need assistance with healing some part of your past, ask the angels to guide you to a great healing center or therapist. Accepting outside help is a wonderful way to love ourselves. Say, "Thank you, my darling angels, for guiding me to the perfect healing center or therapist to help me heal my past. Thank you for helping me find the beauty and blessings in every situation and to see that only love is real."

Prayer for Manifesting Health

Here is a sample prayer that you can use to help manifest perfect health.

Worthiness

"Lord God and my dearest angels, I am worthy of your goodness, your grace, and your blessings. By the simple fact that I exist, I am worthy of perfect health. I am willing to release myself from all negative emotions and false beliefs that no longer serve me and that may be affecting my health. I also forgive those who have trespassed against me as I forgive myself. I know that my will is your will and you only want what is best for me."

Desire

"Dearest angels, it is my greatest desire to experience perfect health."

Trust

"My dearest angels, I trust you completely. I know you have heard my request and you are already working on its fulfillment. I promise you, my dearest angels, that I will follow any divine guidance regarding my health and will accept God's will, whatever it may be."

Imagination

"I reserve at least ten minutes a day to imagine myself experiencing perfect health, and I pretend I already have it."

Gratitude

"Thank you in advance, Lord God and my dearest angels, for the fulfillment of my greatest desire to experience perfect health. Thank you, thank you, thank you."

EXERCISE
Manifesting Health with the Angels

The angels suggest the following exercises to help you with your healing. Ask Archangel Raphael, the healer, to accompany you during this exercise. Archangel Raphael's energy is emerald green and he suggests that we use a green pen to help heal anything we put on paper. He says, "As you write, so it is healed."

Prevention

First, let's take a look at some of the common expressions you use that may be affecting your body and even be causing disease.

Make a list of regular expressions you use to describe what is going on in your life. Here is an example:

Expression	Part of the Body Affected
"I just can't digest what he did!"	Digestive system

Where do you feel any discomfort in your body right now? List any illnesses, pains, discomforts, or diseases you have at the moment.

Can you relate your expressions to your discomfort or disease?

Ask your angels to help you stay aware of your thoughts and expressions that may be harming your health.

Say, "Thank you, my dearest angels, for helping me stay aware of any expressions I have been using that may be affecting my health."

Fear

Fear is one of the main causes of disease. Fear can cause stress, tension, and anxiety, and in the long run, exhaustion or chronic disease. We are mostly afraid of not being loved, of not being lovable, of not being good enough, but we can also be afraid of not having enough, which leads to feelings of financial insecurity.

Ask yourself, "What am I afraid of?"

If such a thing occurred, what would be the worst consequence? How would you handle it?

In this moment, can you change anything in the situation to reduce your fear?

Make an action plan to reduce your fear. This may include saving money, taking courses, taking a vacation, dieting, etc.

There is always a solution to every problem. You can face your fears in your imagination to see that no matter what happens, you will be able to deal with them. Remember, you are not alone. Your angels are near you and want to help. Ask them for solutions and pay attention to the divine signs for the answers.

Say, "Thank you, my dearest angels, for helping me find solutions to reduce my fears. I know you love me and are here for me. There is nothing to fear with you by my side."

Anger

If you feel a strong desire to express any anger or frustration, find a way to physically let go of it, such as through a good workout.

Know that when we are angry at someone else, we are usually angry at ourselves. Are you angry at yourself for putting yourself in a bad situation, for not speaking up or setting healthy boundaries, for letting yourself be taken advantage of, and for not loving and respecting yourself enough? Anger is simply fear disguised. We do these things mostly out of fear of not being loved for who we really are.

Ask the archangels to help you see the situation more clearly, be true to yourself, set healthy boundaries, express yourself, and heal the relationship.

You can say, "Thank you, dearest archangels, for helping me see this situation more clearly. Help me be true to myself and to my needs. Thank you for the strength and confidence to speak my truth and set healthy boundaries. Help me find the courage and the right words to express myself in a loving and firm manner. Help us heal this relationship for the greatest good of all. Thank you, thank you, thank you."

EXERCISE
The Language of Disease

Disease is a sign that we are not at ease with some part of our life. Something is out of sync with who we really are.

Let's look at what your illness or discomfort might really be telling you.

Answer these three important questions:

1. How do I feel physically? Irritated, inflamed, tight, stuck stiff, etc.?

2. How do I feel emotionally about my discomfort? Anxious, panicked, paralyzed, disappointed, scared, nervous, sad, etc.?

3. Do I feel the same way in another area of my life? Like in my family, friendships, work, finances, love life, etc.?

Describe the situation you are experiencing.

Thank your body for the message: "Thank you, body (name the specific part), for your message, your love, and your support. I know that you are my best friend and you only want what is best for me."

If you have any difficulty with this exercise, ask Archangel Raphael to help you understand what you need to know. Say, "Thank you, Archangel Raphael, for helping find the right words to describe my pain and discomfort and for helping see which part of my life I need to heal in order to help heal my body. I know my body is my friend and is lovingly holding on to this pain to help me see it better in my own life. I am willing to look honestly at any situation or relationship that may be affecting my health, and I am willing to let go of any fears, worry, beliefs, or resentment that may be preventing me from experiencing perfect health. Thank you, thank you, thank you."

Healing

Now that you know which area of your life requires more love and attention, you can address it.

Make an action plan to reduce your stress, face your fears, express your needs, forgive others, and do what you need to do to be at peace regarding the situation. Write down what you feel guided to do to bring peace to your mind, body, and spirit.

EXERCISE
Self-Forgiveness

Self-forgiveness is an important part of your healing. Start by making a list of everything you have done or think you did for which you may need to forgive yourself. Ask Archangel Raphael to accompany you during this exercise, and continue to use a green pen.

Is there anything on your list that is really so unforgivable? Is there anything for which you would not forgive someone else? Grant yourself the same forgiveness that you would give to others.

For each thing on your list, write it down, look in the mirror, put your hand on your heart to feel the love, and say this out loud: "I forgive myself for _____. I did my best with the knowledge I had at that time."

EXERCISE

Forgiveness of Others

Forgiving others is essential for your well-being. We do not forgive others for them, but for ourselves. Know that keeping all the anger, shame, and guilt inside of you is only hurting yourself.

Do the following exercise for each person you need to forgive.

Sit in a quiet place and invite Archangel Gabriel (the angel of communication) and Archangel Raphael (the angel of healing) to assist you with this exercise. Continue using a green pen, and know that while you are writing, the situation is being healed. Answer the following questions:

- Whom do you need to forgive (name of the person)?
- How did you feel during and after this event?
- How did this event affect the rest of your life?
- What did you learn from this experience?
- What good came of it?
- What qualities did you develop as a result of this event?
- What is the gift of this transgression? (Continue writing with your green pen, and if you have trouble seeing the good in this situation, ask Archangel Raphael to show it to you.)

Answer each question and finish with a sentence of forgiveness, such as "I understand that you could not have done any better with the knowledge and life experience you had at the time. With the help of my angels, I accept that this event happened and I forgive you. I free myself from all negative emotions related to this event."

Worthiness

Write down your beliefs about health and disease. Here are some examples:

- "Disease is hereditary."
- "My pain is chronic and I just have to live with it."
- "My disease is chronic and I just have to learn to live with it."

For each of your beliefs, ask yourself if this belief is helping you manifest health or not.

For each of your negative beliefs, rewrite the belief and state that you are ready to release it:

- "I release the belief that disease is hereditary."
- "I release the belief that I have to live with this chronic pain."
- "I release the belief I have to live with this chronic disease."

Then create new beliefs in the present tense:

- "My body is an amazing self-healing machine."
- "I am fully capable of assisting and allowing my body to self-heal."
- "I believe in the power of miracles."

Desire

Ask yourself, "How do I really want to feel health-wise?"

Then write down your answer, such as "I desire to feel healthy and energetic, full of life and vitality. I desire to experience perfect health."

Trust

Be open to all the guidance that presents itself to you. Ask your angels to guide you to new healing methods or health practitioners and follow their advice.

Imagination

Imagine that you are already experiencing perfect health. How would you spend your day? What would you be doing right now if you felt energetic and full of vitality? Let yourself imagine how wonderful you would feel and know that these emotions will help you experience health even for a few brief moments. The more you are able to bring yourself into this loving state of calm and peace, the more you are enabling your body to self-heal.

Gratitude

Write down what you are grateful for concerning your health. For example:

- "I am grateful that I am able to walk, see, taste, hear, feel, and smell."
- "I am grateful for _____."

10
MANIFESTING LOVE

"To love is not to look at each other,
it is looking together in the same direction."
—*Antoine de Saint-Exupéry*

Love, love, love! Most of us want to experience true love in our lives. Yes, there are periods when we take time out to heal our heart from past battles, but sooner or later our little heart wants to open up again in hopes of finding that special someone God and the angels have planned just for us. Too often, though, some people lose hope too soon and choose to be content with someone who is not exactly the one whom life had reserved for them, and over time, their inner light dies out. Sometimes we meet someone we think is perfect for us, but they turn out to be all wrong. Others choose to be alone, believing that they will never find the perfect person for them or that they do not need love in their lives. They may feel undeserving of love, lack self-esteem, or have never been able to forget the one who got away, while others simply choose to be alone, happy with the love of family and friends.

Living a great love with a true beloved is one of our greatest desires. Sharing our joys and sorrows with someone with whom we feel safe and secure, evolving and growing beside someone special, can be one of the most enriching and rewarding experiences in life.

The desire to manifest a great love in our life is a choice, and with all choices come responsibilities. We must want to attract love for the right reasons and not just to fill a void inside ourselves or to occupy our time. Each person must have something to bring to the other and to contribute to the relationship. To love someone is, first of all, to love ourselves well. This means to know ourselves, to care for our own needs and desires first, and to be loving toward ourselves.

Know that even if you are in a relationship right now, this chapter can help you improve your current relationship and allow more love into your life.

Before trying to attract a new beloved or heal your current relationship, the angels suggest you take a look at what you have attracted in your life so far, so as not to attract the same type of person or situation in the future. Like attracts like. So if the last person you dated did not have all the qualities you wanted, you probably did not either. We always attract who we are.

What qualities did you attract in the past? Did you have those traits as well? Maybe the other person was afraid of not being loved. Do you have that same fear? If the person was emotionally unavailable, ask yourself if you really are. If the person did not love you or respect you the way you wanted, ask yourself if you love and respect yourself.

It's important to understand that if the person was a narcissist and manipulator, it does not mean that you are also a narcissist and manipulator. You have to look behind the behavior and see why the person is like that. For example, the person may be insecure, lacking real self-esteem and self-confidence. You may be lacking these too, but for you it may translate into you not being able to express yourself and be assertive.

Remember that everything in your life is a reflection of you. This is not an easy thing to admit, but it's true. I have often attracted the same type of person. I always felt that men did not love me and respect me the way I wanted and needed. But over the years, I came to understand that they were merely a reflection of who I was, because if I had loved and respected myself more, I would never have agreed to be in such relationships.

Once you understand that you attract who you are, you can then choose who you wish to be and work on becoming that better person to attract the same into your life. Take, for example, the last three people you dated. Do they have certain personality traits in common? We often keep attracting the same type of person over and over. Can you see how you might have some of those same traits?

If you have difficulty seeing in yourself the traits that you did not like about your ex-partners or do not like about your current partner, ask Archangel Uriel to help you see clearly. He will shed light on any situation that is obscure. Say, "Thank you, Archangel Uriel, for showing me how the traits I see in others, I have in myself or have had them in the past."

I did this exercise. I made a list of what I did not like in the other person, and I asked Archangel Uriel to show me examples of moments when I had those traits in me. It did not take long for the memories to resurface, and I must admit that I did attract who I was. What I did not like about the other person, I did not like about myself.

For example, I saw most of my exes as controlling and manipulative and as people who did not respect and love me the way I wanted. Archangel Uriel helped me see that they lacked self-esteem and self-confidence and showed me that I, too, was lacking those qualities. I had difficulty expressing myself for fear of not being heard, understood, and loved. I also tried to manipulate and control things in my own way out of fear of not being loved for who I was, rather than expressing myself honestly with confidence, and I know that this fear of being assertive comes from my childhood. My exes also had the same fears as me. We were afraid of not being loved, and that's what we attracted in each other.

Are you willing to change what you do not like about yourself? You cannot change another person. You can only work on you. When you change yourself, the next person who comes into your life will be different, or even the person you are with now will change. When you admit who you really are, recognizing the traits that no longer serve you and that you are willing to work on, only then will you no longer attract the same type of person or situation.

Ask Archangel Raphael to help you:

"Dear Archangel Raphael, I deeply desire to change the following traits I have in myself: _____. Please help me free myself from these traits and assist me in transforming them into more positive qualities. I forgive myself for _____. I promise to love and respect myself more. I promise to be my best friend. Thank you for helping me honor who I really am. Thank you, thank you, thank you."

From my own personal experience, each unhealthy relationship I have experienced has taught me to love myself more, set healthy boundaries, and be more assertive. We need to be free to be ourselves, and we are the only ones who can give ourselves that freedom.

God and the angels want you to be happy. They want you to experience healthy and loving relationships. The most important relationship you will ever have is with yourself. We need to learn to love ourselves well first before we can really love another person.

Manifesting Love

Worthiness

If you did not do the exercise about self-esteem and self-confidence that appears at the beginning of chapter 7, I strongly recommend that you do so now before continuing. We attract who we are, so it is important to be the best version of yourself to attract the best version of your beloved. The more you love yourself, the more you will attract a person who loves himself (or herself) and will love you back. Even if you are currently in a relationship, you can start to love yourself more by honoring your needs and desires, setting healthy boundaries, and being more assertive.

The angels are here to help you love yourself more and prepare you for this great love. They want you to discover a great truth: You are perfect just as you are, and you deserve the very best life has to offer, including great love. The angels say that our biggest obstacle is that we do not see and recognize the perfect, magnificent being we really are. Seeing ourselves as anything but perfect is what prevents us from experiencing great love. Being perfect does not mean we have it all together; it simply means that underneath all of our pain we have accumulated over the years, our soul is perfect, just like the soul of a newborn baby. The angels invite us to see our perfection beneath all those layers of pain.

Know that you are worthy of God and the angels' blessings, mercy, and goodness. You are worthy simply because you exist.

PREPARING FOR LOVE

Throughout the years, the angels have given me many ideas on how to prepare ourselves for this great love. They say that if we really want to attract love into our life, we must prepare our space and our heart to receive it. When you receive your friends, don't you clean your house? It is the same for your beloved. Wouldn't you want your new partner to be emotionally healed from their past and be emotionally available to you? The angels invite you to do the same to prepare yourself ceremoniously for your beloved. I choose to use the term *beloved* instead of *soul mate* because we all need to remember to love well and to be loved.

PHYSICAL CLEANING

First we must physically clean up our life. This means cleaning out our closets, cupboards, and bathrooms. Make sure positive energy flows well in your home, and make room for your beloved. If your home or apartment is too cluttered, your beloved will have difficulty imagining themselves in your life. You must prepare your love nest for your beloved, and you must feel comfortable in your environment as well. When energy flows well in your life and in your home, you are happier and lighter and you feel better about yourself, which makes you more attractive.

Clear out all those old clothes you no longer wear or that no longer fit. Let go of stuff that has too many memories of past relationships attached to it. Clear out your photo albums, your computer, even your jewelry box. Make space for the new. Declutter your home, your office, and your life. Simplify your life. Give away what you no longer need or use. Honor your things by allowing them to serve another.

While you are cleaning out your closets, ask yourself if you are due for a new, updated look. Go ahead and buy yourself a few new outfits and new lingerie. Show the angels that you have faith in them by taking bold steps.

They also suggest you prepare your body. Get your hair done regularly, pamper yourself, get into an exercise program, and eat better. All of these things will help you feel better about yourself and feel more attractive.

EMOTIONAL CLEARING

Free your heart and mind of any sadness, resentment, and anger you may have regarding your past lovers. Forgive them and forgive yourself for anything you have experienced. Know that it was simply an experience to teach you what you needed to know. There are no mistakes, only lessons. Through relationships, we learn how to love. And your past partners helped you love yourself more.

Many people continue to think and talk about their exes long after they are gone. Refrain from thinking and talking about your exes. Instead, start dreaming of a new beloved and what you would like to experience in a new relationship. It's important to focus on the future and have positive expectations.

If you are still feeling sorrow, bitterness, or anger about a past relationship, ask Archangel Raphael to help you heal these emotions. Pour your heart out once and for all on paper and leave the past in the past. Try to understand what these past relationships have taught you about yourself and what lessons you needed to learn.

Say, "Thank you, Archangel Raphael, for helping me heal my heart from past relationships. I know that they did the best they could with what they knew. I forgive them and I forgive myself. I am ready to release any negative emotions and memories related to my past lovers. I am free and they are free to move forward. I send them love and I love myself. Thank you, thank you, thank you."

BELIEFS

The angels also suggest that you be conscious and aware of your beliefs about love. Your thoughts create. If you believe that all the good men are taken, that no one exists for you, that you do not deserve to be loved, or that no one could really love you the way you would like them to, then that is what you will create and attract in your life. For each one of your beliefs, ask yourself if the belief is drawing love to you or pushing love away. Ask Archangel Raphael to help you release any negative beliefs. Say, "Thank you, Archangel Raphael, for helping me release any negative beliefs I have about love."

Desire

The angels suggest you ask yourself what do you really desire to experience in your love life. This is an important question. Many people do not think about what they want to experience in their relationship; they just want to be in love. But know that love is a responsibility, like having a child or a pet is a responsibility. A relationship requires an investment of time and energy. Ask yourself if you really have the time and energy for a new relationship or if you are looking to fill a void. It is very painful to wake up in a relationship in which you still feel empty inside. Another person cannot fulfill our void, and it is not their responsibility to do so. We all have to fill up our own selves by loving ourselves first and by healing our past. We are also responsible for what we bring to the relationship with our beloved. It is important to be well with ourselves and to be emotionally healed and available.

If you want a relationship, make sure you have something to bring to it. You must not want someone in your life simply as a distraction and to occupy your time. This is also a very big burden to put on another person. This is not love but dependence, and those relationships rarely last and are very unhealthy. They only end up hurting both people involved. Unfortunately, we all see and experience relationships like these.

True love is when two people are complete, feel good about themselves, love their lives and simply want to share that with another person.

So first, determine what you would like to experience in love. Here are a few examples:

- • "I desire to grow and evolve in love with my beloved."
- • "I desire to be free to be myself completely with my beloved."
- • "I wish to experience passion, trust, respect, and admiration with my beloved."
- • "I wish to experience a deep soul connection with my beloved, my best friend."
- • "I wish to grow into the best person I can be and allow my beloved to be all that he (or she) wishes to be as well."

Trust

Once you have established what you would like to experience in your new or existing relationship, stay open to, follow, and trust any guidance that comes to you.

If you are in an existing relationship, you may be guided to be more compassionate, more understanding and more patient with your beloved, or you may be guided to do more loving things for yourself. You may also feel a new desire to take a class together, do some outdoor activities with your partner, or even spend more quality time with your friends.

If you are single, you may be guided to join a group, accept invitations from friends, and leave the house. Take action, but do not try to control the results. Be patient. Keep the faith. Remain calm and receptive so that you may experience real love even faster.

The angels suggest you stay open to any new person who may be presented to you and know that it is possible that the angel's image of your new beloved may differ from yours. Stay open and follow your intuition and the signs. Leave the "how" to the angels. They know how to orchestrate this divine encounter or help you experience more love in your life. Do not worry about how and when you will meet your beloved. Have absolute faith that the angels are taking care of it. Focus on taking small guided steps to attracting this great love, or creating it if you already have a beloved. You have already learned how to see, feel, hear, and know the signs. Now is the time to follow them.

Also stay very aware of and trust your feelings. You may meet someone who has all the qualities you desire in a person, but you feel something is off. Listen to your gut feelings. The angels speak to you through your clairsentience, so trust any sensations that may indicate that the person is all wrong. We have all made bad choices in the past; just remember that you can always change your mind. You have free will and the angels want you to be happy. They will simply guide you to a person who is better suited for you. There are no mistakes, only experiences. Each relationship brings us one step closer to experiencing true love.

If you are in an unhealthy or abusive relationship right now, you can pray to God and the angels to help you have the courage and strength to leave.

Say, "Dear God and my darling angels, thank you for the courage and strength to do what I know is right in my heart. Help me be firm and assertive and walk away from this unhealthy relationship. I know you are with me, are protecting me, and will fully support me through this transition. I know that you are my Source and that you will provide for me. I am not alone. Thank you, thank you, thank you."

Imagination

The angels strongly suggest we use our imagination more. So imagine that you are already experiencing love in your life. Imagine that your beloved is already present. How would your life be different if your beloved was already there beside you or you were already experiencing the kind of love you want to live with your present partner?

Every morning and evening, imagine how you wish to experience this great love. When you wake up in the morning, while you are still in bed, imagine how you wish to be as a couple. Imagine what you would say to your beloved and what you would do together. Imagine a complete day with your beloved. Pretend that the person is already there, sleeping by your side. Look your beloved in the eye and tell them how much you love them, how happy you are to have found them. Converse with your beloved and feel their presence in your life.

Throughout the day, pretend that your beloved is with you. What would you talk about? What kind of activities would you do together? Do those things. Go on an excursion, go for a carriage ride, buy yourself flowers, or even go eat at a restaurant with your imaginary beloved. If you keep imagining your new beloved beside you, you will feel so happy and loved that love will have no choice but to find you!

Pretending that love is already in your life and knowing deep in your heart that it is on the way will make you feel so happy that you will no longer feel the urgency for that person to show up. You will develop faith. You will just know your beloved is on the way. Pretending to be in love will expand your heart, and you will feel the love growing inside you. And it is this feeling of love inside that will attract your beloved to you even sooner.

Gratitude

Be grateful in advance for all the love and the new beloved you are attracting to you. Be grateful for everything you've ever experienced in the name of love and for all the lessons you've learned so far. Send love to all your ex-lovers and your present partner, if you have one, and thank them for having come into your life. Here are a few examples:

- "Thank you, God and the angels, for all the people who have passed through my life and have taught me so much about love, which has helped me grow and love myself."

- "Thank you, God and the angels, for helping me send love to all the people from my past, all of my friends who are experiencing love or also wish to meet their beloved. I wish that all of us could experience great love."

- "Thank you, God and the angels, for bringing me the perfect person."

- "Thank you, God and the angels, for helping my partner and me experience a deeper and more meaningful love."

- "Thank you, God and the angels, for _____. Thank you, thank you, thank you!"

Manifesting Your Beloved

If your heart is free from the past and open to love, the angels suggest you start a conversation with your beloved. He (or she) already exists. He is alive. He may be experiencing a broken heart or is preparing to meet you. Speak to him, soul to soul. Tell him that you are looking forward to meeting him in person, but you are content to simply speak with his soul today. Send him peace, love, and friendship. Feel the love in your heart that you already have for him and him for you.

Talk with your beloved every day, as if he is already there. Tell him about your day, your dreams, and your hopes.

Do not imagine a specific person whom you already know. You must stay open to meeting the perfect person for you and remember that your idea of the perfect person may differ from the angel's.

Trust that God and the angels know what is best for you. Allow them the freedom to orchestrate this wonderful divine encounter. You will not be disappointed. For example, I recommended this process to my friend Kim. She set out one morning for a walk on an icy river. In the middle of the river, she lay on a small outcrop of grass where she started talking to her soul mate and told him she was eager to meet him in person. She sent him a lot of love, hoping he would find her soon.

A week later, she went to Toronto with a friend for a wedding. Her friend told her, "I have someone I would like you to meet!" Upon their arrival, a second friend said the same thing. While she was sitting in the living room, a man appeared in the doorway. As soon as they saw each other, her heart skipped a beat. They looked into each other's eyes and felt an immediate attraction. They spent the entire evening talking and getting to know each other.

The following week, he came to visit her at home. In the morning, they left together to take a walk on the river. He headed straight toward the same patch of grass and lay down in the exact same spot where she had started her conversation with him the week before. He looked into her eyes and flashed a beautiful smile. She knew at that moment that this was the man she had invited into her life.

Divine Timing

The angels say that anyone destined to meet their beloved will meet them when they are ready. Many of us do not find the right person simply because we settle too fast for the wrong person, lose hope, and choose to stay in the relationship, thinking that it's the best we can do.

The angels recommend that you spend your time loving yourself while waiting for the arrival of your beloved. Get out and have fun, see your friends, join groups, and try out new activities. Work on being the best version of you. Focus on being happy and fulfilling your life's mission. Do what brings you joy. The more you love yourself and your life, the less needy you will be and the quicker you will attract a great person like yourself.

Also, continue to be grateful to God and the angels and to your future beloved for their presence in your life. Your beloved is already part of your journey; it is only a matter of time before this person shows up. On a soul level, you already know each other.

For those of you who have already manifested a divine relationship, remember to be grateful every day for the presence of your beloved and celebrate the joy and wholeness that only the right beloved can bring you.

Prayer for Manifesting Love

Here is a sample prayer that you can use to help manifest more love in your life.

Worthiness

"Lord God, I am worthy of your goodness, your grace, and your blessings. I know that my will is your will and you only want what is best for me. By the simple fact that I exist, I am worthy of love. I free myself from all negative emotions and false beliefs about love that do not serve me. I forgive all my former partners (and my present partner) who have trespassed against me and I forgive myself all trespasses I have done unto them. I know my will is your will and you only want what is in my highest good."

Desire

"Dearest angels, I really desire to experience great love. I desire to grow and evolve in love with my beloved, to be completely free to be myself. I wish to experience passion, trust, respect, admiration, and a deep soul connection with my beloved. I want to be the best person I can be in life and also allow my beloved to be all that they choose to be and become."

Trust

"My dearest angels, I trust you completely. I know you have heard my request and you are already working on its fulfillment. I promise you, my dear angels, that I will follow your divine guidance."

Imagination

I reserve at least ten minutes a day to imagine what it is I desire in a relationship, and I pretend I already have it.

Gratitude

"Thank you in advance, Lord God and my dearest angels, for bringing me the perfect person. I am grateful for all the people who have come into my life and taught me so much about love, which helped me grow and love myself more. Thank you for helping me send love to all the people from my past and all my friends who are experiencing love or wishing to meet their beloved. I wish that we could all experience this great love. Thank you, God and my dearest angels, in advance for the fulfillment of my greatest desire to experience a great love. Thank you, thank you, thank you."

EXERCISE
Preparing to Manifest Love

This exercise will help you prepare to manifest a new love in your life or help you heal the relationship you already have.

First, let's look at what you did not like about your past partners or even your present partner and how you might have some of those same traits. Remember, we attract who we are.

For each of your ex-partners, make a list of what you did not like about them, and take an honest look at yourself to see if have those same traits.

If you have difficulty seeing in yourself the traits that you did not like about your ex-partners or your current partner, ask Archangel Uriel to help you see clearly. He will shed light on any situation that is obscure. Say, "Thank you, Archangel Uriel, for showing me how the traits I see in others, I have in myself or have had them in the past."

Next, ask Archangel Raphael to help you transform these traits into more positive qualities:

"Dear Archangel Raphael, I deeply desire to change the following traits I have in myself: _____. Please help me free myself from these traits and assist me in transforming them into more positive qualities. I forgive myself for _____. I promise to love and respect myself more. I promise to be my best friend. Thank you for helping me honor who I really am. Thank you, thank you, thank you."

Now that you have acknowledged having the traits that you do not like in others, you can work on transforming those negative aspects into positive qualities by loving and honoring who you really are.

EXERCISE
Manifesting Love

To attract love into your life, you will use the same steps we discussed in the previous chapter: worthiness, desire, trust, imagination, and gratitude.

Worthiness

If you did not do the exercise about self-esteem and self-confidence that appears at the beginning of chapter 7, I strongly recommend that you do so now before continuing. The more we love ourselves, the more we will attract to us a person who loves himself (or herself) and who can really love us in return.

PHYSICAL CLEANING

The angels say it is important to physically clean up our life. This means cleaning out our closets, cupboards, and bathrooms. They say that energy should flow well in our home. We all feel better after cleaning our house. It uplifts our spirit and gives us more energy. If your home or apartment is too cluttered, your beloved will have difficulty imagining themselves in your life. Make room for your beloved and prepare your love nest. Make it so it is comfortable for both of you.

EMOTIONAL CLEARING

Free your heart and mind of any sadness, resentment, and anger you may have regarding your past lovers. Forgive them and forgive yourself for anything you have experienced. Know that it was simply an experience to teach you what you needed to know. There are no mistakes, only lessons.

Through relationships, we learn how to love better. Each past partner helped you love yourself more.

The angels say it is important to let go of your past by no longer talking or thinking about your ex. Focus on the future and the wonderful new person you wish to attract and what you would like to experience. It's important to have positive expectations.

If you are still feeling sorrow, bitterness, or anger about a past relationship, ask Archangel Raphael to help you heal these emotions.

Pour your heart out once and for all through journaling and leave the past in the past. Use a green ink pen. Try to see what these past relationships have taught you about yourself.

For each one of your exes, end with a sentence of forgiveness, such as "I understand that you could not have done any better with the knowledge and life experience you had at the time. With the help of my angels, I accept the fact that we lived through this experience and I forgive us both. I free myself of all negative emotions related to this relationship."

BELIEFS

Beliefs become a self-fulfilling prophecy. Always be conscious and aware of your beliefs about love. Your thoughts create. If you believe that all the good men are taken, that no one exists for you, that you do not deserve to be loved, or that no one could really love you the way you would like them to, then that is what you will experience.

Write down your beliefs about love. For example: "All the good men (or women) are taken."

For each one of your beliefs, ask yourself if the belief is drawing love to you or pushing love away. Ask Archangel Raphael to help you release any negative beliefs.

Rewrite each belief you are ready to release. For example: "I release the belief that all the good men (or women) are taken."

Desire

What do you really desire to experience in your love life? This is a very important question.

So first, write down what you would like to experience in love. Here are a few examples:

+ "I desire to grow and evolve in love with my beloved."
+ "I desire to be free to be myself completely with my beloved."
+ "I wish to experience passion, trust, respect, and admiration with my beloved."
+ "I wish to experience a deep soul connection with my beloved, my best friend."
+ "I wish to be the best person I can be and allow my beloved to be everything they wish to be too."

Trust

Once you have established what you would like to experience in your relationship, stay open to all the possibilities and opportunities that will come to you. It is possible that the image you have of love differs from the divine's. Stay open and trust. Follow your intuition and the divine signs. Leave the "how" to the angels. They know how to orchestrate this divine encounter. Do not worry about how and when you will meet your beloved. Have absolute faith that the angels are taking care of it. Focus on taking small guided steps to attracting this great love. You already learned how to see, feel, hear, and know the signs. Now is the time to follow them. Join a group, accept invitations from friends, and get out of the house. Take action, but do not try to control the results. Be patient. Keep the faith. Remain calm and receptive so your beloved will arrive faster. Note the actions you feel guided to take.

Imagination

Imagine that your beloved is already present in your life. Imagine how your life would be different if this person was already there. How would you live with this love in your day-to-day life?

Describe in your journal your dream life with your beloved.

Every morning and evening, imagine how you wish to experience this great love. Throughout the day, pretend that your beloved is with you. Pretending that love is already in your life will make you feel so happy that you will no longer feel the urgency for that someone special to arrive.

The more you imagine that your beloved is already there, the more love you will feel and the sooner love will find you.

Gratitude

Be grateful in advance for all the love and the new beloved you are attracting to you. Be grateful for everything you've ever experienced in the name of love and for all the lessons you have learned so far. Send love to all your ex-lovers and thank them for having come into your life. Here are some examples:

- "Thank you, God and the angels, for bringing me the perfect person."
- "Thank you, God and the angels, for all the people who have passed through my life and have taught me so much about love, which helped me grow and love myself."
- "Thank you, God and the angels, for helping me send love to all the people from my past and all of my friends who are experiencing love or who wish to meet their beloved. I wish that all of us could experience great love."
- "Thank you, God and the angels, for_____. Thank you, thank you, thank you!"

11

MANIFESTING EMPLOYMENT

"When you want something,
all the universe conspires in helping you to achieve it."
—*Paulo Coelho*

There may come a time in life when we are called to change jobs or careers. Maybe we are laid off or simply feel the need or a deep desire to make a change in our work life. Change is a natural process of life. Nothing ever stays the same, no matter how much we want it to. Sometimes, if we are living in fear, we'll be tempted to stay where we are despite the inner nudging to move on, but life will always find a way to get us on the path of change. For example, you may no longer feel happy where you are, you start to experience problems with your boss or coworkers, or maybe you fall ill. Rest assured that life is speaking to you and is saying, "There is something better for you. Open your arms wide to receive."

When you find yourself out of work or feeling a deep desire for change, know that God and the angels have something better for you and it is your faith in them and your belief in their goodness that will help you attract something better. Do not be afraid. When you live in fear, you are tempted to stay where you are or perhaps show a tolerance for unpleasant situations that may eventually make you ill. Know that there is something special just for you. Give the angels a chance to bring it to you.

Whether you believe in angels or not, I am convinced that the universe, God, Spirit—call it what you want—is working behind the scenes for you. If you pay attention to the signs, your intuition and your gut feelings, you will see that life always brings you the right job or opportunity at the perfect time. Your life is perfectly orchestrated. And if you stop long enough to observe, you will see the perfection and beauty in the tapestry of your life.

See the perfection and beauty in the tapestry of your life.

Life is like a river. Allow yourself to flow with life and let it guide you to exactly where you need to be. The angels say that there are times when you have to choose what you want, but the course, in general, has already been traced. For example, the angels say to imagine you are going down a river and you come upon a fork. You can go left or go right. One direction may look easier at the outset but become more difficult as you flow downstream. The other way may look arduous at the beginning but quickly turn into a nice, easy ride. But looking at it from where you are, you cannot see down the river. You have to make a choice. The angels suggest you go inside and ask them for guidance. Feel what is best for you. Know that there are no mistakes, only experiences.

Many people stay in jobs in which they are no longer happy. You always thought you would stay there for your entire career, but now, suddenly, things are not as perfect as before. You no longer have the support you once had and you notice that the fundamental values of your employer are no longer consistent with yours. These may be signs that it is time to move on. Do not stay at a job where you are no longer well. Do not stay for the money or out of fear that there is nothing better for you, and do not stay for the retirement plan. Don't put off your joy now in the hopes of being happy once you retire. Know that some people who put off their happiness until retirement never get to see it. Do what makes you happy today, and the joy you bring to your everyday life will be what actually prolongs your life.

I know a man who talked about retirement his whole life. Every day he counted down the number of days he had left until he would reach his retirement on his sixtieth birthday. Two years before his retirement, he developed a brain tumor. The day he was supposed to retire, he was actually lying in bed waiting to die in the very hospital where he had worked his whole life.

Back in my early twenties, many of my friends worked for an airline company that closed its doors. I was amazed at how the people who were unhappy, who wanted to make a change but were afraid to leave, found themselves out of work, and the people who loved their job were immediately hired by the competition. I could see how God and the angels were working their magic. They were helping these friends move out of their comfort zones and into new jobs and new opportunities. Sometimes when we are afraid of making a move that we know we should make, God and the angels make it for us. Trust that there is something better for you. They only want what is best for you. God loves you. Life loves you. So trust that everything is always working for you and not against you. God and the angels have always been there for you in the past, have they not? They have supported you thus far, so know that they will continue to do so.

When life suddenly no longer goes the way you want, I call this "divine discontent." It is a sign that you need to change something in your life. Many people choose to fight to keep things as they were before. The angels encourage you to stop fighting and stop resisting change. The more you resist change, the more difficult life will become. Life may simply have a different plan for you. Just let go of your preconceived ideas about what you want and allow something new to unfold. You may be pleasantly surprised.

Divine discontent is a sign that you need to change something in your life. I knew a lady who started to experience a difficult situation in her workplace with her boss. It started off with him undermining her work and judgment. She retaliated by taking extended sick leave. When she returned, he made life so difficult for her that she actually became ill and depressed. She ended up taking pills for her depression and alcohol to numb her pain even further. She was determined to stick it out until she retired. The situation became so unbearable for everyone that she eventually was given an early retirement after fighting for ten years. That kind of stress will take a toll on a person and may even shorten their life. Often we stay in unbearable situations because we resist change, and only God and the angels know what wonderful opportunities this lady missed out on.

When it comes to fighting to keep your job in the workplace, choose your battles wisely. You may say to me, "But in years past, people fought to improve their working conditions." Yes, the movements in the 1970s were needed to improve the working conditions of women and workers in general, to reduce the injustices suffered by the oppressed groups, but these people did not remain *victims*. They created the future they wanted. How do you know whether or not to fight? Listen to your inner voice. Does this battle give you energy or does it simply exhaust you? Does it help others? Are your demands fair and just?

There are no victims in life, only creators.

Sometimes there are battles that are important to fight to improve the lives of all, but if the battle is only for you, for your wounded ego, it is probably not worth the trouble. You will hurt yourself physically, emotionally, psychologically, and spiritually, while God and the angels just wanted to give you something better. However, to receive it, you must be open, know that you are worthy, believe that there is something better waiting for you, and open yourself up to receive it.

The angels want you to know that the only thing that matters in this life is your happiness in the present moment. Do everything you can do to be happy now and know that tomorrow will care for itself.

A very well-respected author and coach I know started a business with another person after losing her job. Once the business was all set up, her business partner no longer wanted to work with her and asked to leave. She was devastated. She cried for a whole week. She prayed for guidance and then felt an urge to sit down and write. She remembered that when she was young, she used to really enjoy writing. She started to write little essays about learning to love ourselves better and posted them on social media. These essays eventually became a book that she self-published, and within a few months it became a bestseller. There are blessings in every situation. If we take the time to pray to our angels and ask for guidance and find the courage to follow it, what may seem like a dire situation may turn out to be the biggest blessing you could ever imagine.

Beliefs

Many people believe they do not deserve a better job because they feel they do not have enough education or experience, they are too young or too old, or they simply lack self-confidence. Other people believe that they must work hard to get a job, by passing all sorts of tests and interviews, for example. Remember that you attract what you believe. I have always believed that life is supposed to be easy, that opportunities that are meant for me will come easily, without the need to jump through hoops, and this is what I have experienced.

What are your beliefs about work? Are they serving you well?

I have often been led to the perfect job for me. I have sometimes been led to jobs that were not meant for me, but I trusted my gut feeling and turned them down when I sensed they were inappropriate. Since my early twenties, I have sensed and noticed that "something greater than me" was taking care of me. I feel that there is a divine force leading me on a certain path, to the right places and people at the perfect time. I believe it is so for everyone.

When I lived in Ontario, I was unhappy in my work. I felt intimidated by the person who supervised me. During a consultation with a friend, the angels told me to leave my job. At first I was stunned. I thought, "How will I survive?" I had applied for other jobs elsewhere, but no doors were opening. No longer able to continue, I decided to take a leave without pay for one year in January 2005. I had no money and no savings, but I knew I had to leave. A month later, I woke up with a vision of my mother. I felt guided to visit her. That trip took me to Sept-Îles, Quebec, where I experienced the most wonderful week with my mom and friends. Upon my return to Ontario, I knew I was supposed to move closer to them.

One day after my move, I was driving down the boulevard and I heard someone on the radio speaking about a job. I heard only a few words that described the position and I thought, "Ah! That would be the perfect job for me!" I was leaving the next day on a trip with my mother and did not have time to look into the position.

Upon my return, one Monday morning, I told my boyfriend, "I am ready to go to work!" It had been five months since my leave from Ontario and I felt the need to be useful. The next day, I called my aunt who worked for the government to wish her happy birthday, but she was not there, so I left a message on her answering machine. On Thursday, she returned my call and said that she believed there was a job opportunity for me in her office, and she gave me the contact information of the person to call. I immediately sent him my resume. Without even meeting me, he called me the very next morning to inform me that I could start work the following Monday. When I arrived at the office, I was directed to my cubicle and given the job description. To my amazement, I saw that it was the exact position I had heard about on the radio.

God and the angels have always looked after me, and I believe they do this for all of us. I followed all the signs. I had the courage to leave my job when I had no money saved. The angels brought me what I needed to survive. I did not spend all of my time looking for another job either. I felt the need to travel, to care for myself, and to rest. When I felt ready to work, I believed that something would show up and I stayed open to all of the possibilities. I trusted, I believed, and I received. These are the steps to manifest a job.

Sometimes you are in a job but the environment or the atmosphere is not quite what you want. Ask your angels to help you improve your situation. For example, say something like, "Dear angels, please improve my work environment, and this for the greatest good of all!" A few years back, I recommended this strategy to a friend who was having a difficult time fitting in with her new colleagues. A month later, all of her colleagues were transferred to another department and a new team joined her.

The other day this same friend told me that there was a lady who was very loud working near her cubicle. She thought of what I had suggested before and how well it had worked, so she prayed to the angels again. Two days later she received an email stating that two new positions had been created that entailed a few changes in the office. The loud lady was given this new assignment and was transferred down the hall.

Whatever you wish to change, whether it be your career, your job, your environment, or the atmosphere at work, remember that you are not alone. God and the angels support you in all that you do.

God and the angels support you in all that you do.

Feel worthy of having something better in your work life, decide what you really want, and open yourself to all the possibilities. Imagine how you want to feel and what you desire to experience, and thank the angels in advance for the miracle that is about to happen.

You have the right to be happy in your work, and the angels want you to be happy too. So give them a chance to help you create something new and more connected with who you really are. Follow the signs, listen to your intuition, and have the courage to hope for something better and to make necessary changes. Something better exists. It is up to you to open your arms and heart to receive it.

Prayer for Manifesting Employment

Here is a sample prayer that will assist you in manifesting new and better employment.

Worthiness

"Lord God, I am worthy of your goodness, your grace, and your blessings. I know that the perfect job or career for me exists and is waiting for me. Even if there are job cuts, I know there is one perfect job reserved just for me. I know that my will is your will and you only want what is best for me."

Desire

"Dearest angels, I deeply desire a significant new job that pays very well, reflects my deepest values, and allows me to make the most of my qualities and skills, and where harmony reigns between my supervisors, my colleagues, my clients and me."

Trust

"My dearest angels, if this desire is in agreement with your divine plan for me, is for my highest and greatest good and that of others, I ask that you bring me this new job soon. Dear God and my loving angels, I trust you completely. I know you have heard my request and you are already working on its fulfillment. I promise you that I will follow your divine guidance. I will remain open to and follow all the signs that you send my way."

Imagination

I reserve at least ten minutes a day to imagine my dream job. I pretend I am already living it. I feel the joy, love, and wholeness that this new job brings.

Gratitude

"Thank you in advance, Lord God and my dearest angels, for this new significant job that pays very well, reflects my deepest values, and allows me to put my qualities and skills to good use, and where harmony reigns between my supervisors, my colleagues, my clients, and me. I am grateful that you have always guided me toward the perfect job and have always provided me with a good wage. Thank you for this new timely job that suits me perfectly! Thank you, thank you, thank you."

EXERCISE
Manifesting Employment

The best way to manifest a new job is to believe that one exists, and the best way to manifest a new, passionate career is to listen to the special calling that God and the angels have planted in your heart.

Know that you are worthy of the best life has to offer, and let go of any fears and doubts that may be holding you back. Release any old beliefs that no longer serve you. Know what you want in your heart. Pray boldly when you ask God and the angels to help you, and stay in gratitude, knowing the new job is on its way.

Worthiness

Write down your beliefs about manifesting a job. Here are some examples:

+ "I have to work hard to find a job."
+ "I have to be highly educated to have a good-paying job."
+ "There are so many job cuts now. I'll never find a job."

For each of your beliefs, ask yourself if this belief is helping you attract a job or not.

For each of your negative beliefs, rewrite it and state that you are ready to release it:

+ "I release the belief that I have to work hard to find a job."
+ "I release the belief that I must be highly educated to have a good-paying job."

+ "I release the belief that because there are so many job cuts, I'll never find a job."

Now create new beliefs in the present tense:

+ "The perfect job for me exists and is waiting for me."
+ "I am deserving of a very good wage."
+ "Despite job cuts, there is a perfect job that exists for me."

Desire

Ask yourself, "What do I really want in a new job to be happy?" For example:

+ "I would like a significant new job that reflects my deepest values, pays very well, and allows me to make the most of my qualities and skills, and where harmony reigns between my supervisors, my colleagues, my clients, and myself."

Trust

Be open to all opportunities that are presented to you. Ask your angels to guide you to this new employment and follow the divine signs.

Imagination

Imagine that you are already working at your ideal job or in your perfect career. Are you in an office, working outside, or out on the road? Are you traveling? What kind of people do you work with? Are they friendly? How do you feel in this new job? How does it differ from your past employment?

Describe what it would be like to live a full day in your ideal job or career.

Gratitude

Write down what you are grateful for concerning employ-ment. For example:

+ "I am grateful that I am always guided toward the perfect job for me."
+ "I am grateful for always having had a good wage."

12

MANIFESTING ABUNDANCE

"Happiness exists. It is in love, health, peace, material comforts, art, nature, and in thousands of other locations."
—Michele Morgan

What exactly is abundance? According to the Oxford Dictionary, it means "plentifulness of the good things of life; prosperity."

The good things in life are not necessarily material. For some of us, it may be simple pleasures, such as enjoying a picnic with loved ones, experiencing an amusement park, sailing on the ocean, eating an exquisite meal in a fine restaurant, or simply relaxing at the beach.

I believe most of us desire to experience at least a certain level of abundance and prosperity. Most people desire a comfortable life where they can afford a nice place to live and to pay their bills and feed and clothe their kids.

Abundance is not necessarily money. Abundance can be time, energy, friends, relationships, love, joy, ideas, and opportunities.

We live in an era of extreme abundance compared to our grandparents and great-grandparents. In their day, they did not have all the choices and opportunities we have today. Most of them did not have a great career or a big house. Clothes were often passed down from the oldest to the youngest and there was no waste. Most families had only a few bedrooms, and many of the children slept in the same bed. My mother told me that she shared her room with her aunt, and her brother slept on a little bed in the hallway. She did not have a wardrobe like she has now, but only a nail on the back of her room door for her clothes. They did not have the career choices we have today. Today, we can be, do, and have almost anything we desire.

You probably already live in abundance, but maybe you are so used to seeing it that you do not even realize it. Take a moment to look around you. You surely have some abundance in your life. You have family, friends, and great colleagues. You possibly have a husband or a wife and children. You have career opportunities, the ability to travel around the world, to really choose what you want to experience in your life. You have a myriad of choices today.

So you see that abundance already exists around us. We are the generation that is living with the most abundance in our society.

The angels say that money alone does not bring happiness. A person who has a million dollars in their account does not necessarily have abundance in their life. There may be no love or friendship or true meaning to their life. They may be poor in spirit. Money alone is not abundance.

So how can we have more of the good things in life? The angels say the best way to manifest more abundance, more good things in life, is to start by respecting, honoring, and being grateful for what we already have and share it with others.

Attracting Abundance

Respect and Honor

The angels say it is important to honor and respect what we already have to attract even more. We are encouraged to care for the things we have. For example, if you have an old car, you can keep it clean and in good working order. You may have a simple house right now and desire a larger one, so take good care of the one you have. Honor and respect it by keeping it well maintained and in good shape.

If you are a parent, the angels tell me that if your child does not take good care of what they have right now, you may not feel inclined to give them something better. If your child has an old iPad or laptop that they leave on the floor where someone could step on it, you would not feel like getting them a more recent one. If your child has an old bike that they leave in the driveway, you will not feel like buying them a new bike. If they don't take care of what they have, they will probably not care for something better or more precious. It is the same way with us. The angels say, "Take good care of what you have and then we'll entrust you with even more." They say that the same goes for time, money, energy, ideas, and opportunities.

Respect and honor your time. Are you using your time on earth wisely? Are you making the most of every hour given to you in the day, or are you wasting it watching mindless television? The angels suggest you schedule your time in such a way as to have a balanced life. Take time to learn something new, improve your skills, work on your dreams, be with your loved ones, take care of your body, feed your mind, and nourish your spirit.

Are you handling your money wisely? Do you treat your cash with respect, or do you crumble it in your pocket? Do you keep it neatly in a nice purse? Are you using your energy wisely? Do you give all your energy to others without taking the time to fill yourself up? Do you waste your energy surfing the Internet? The angels suggest you put first things first. Build up your energy by exercising, eating right, and working on your dreams. Then you can share the extra energy you have with others. The angels ask whether you are developing the ideas they are sending you or are brushing them off, thinking that you can't do those things? Do you embrace the opportunities that are presented to you, or do you shy away from them? The angels want you to respect and honor the abundance of time, energy, ideas, and opportunities you already have, and they promise they will bring you more.

The same is true for our material things. Native Americans believe that everything is sacred and that everything has a reason for being, just like us. It is important that each thing that exists fulfill its purpose, its reason for being. For example, if we have an item in our life that is not useful, we should give it to someone who will honor its purpose. We are afraid to let go of things, thinking, "I might need it one day when the other one breaks down." That is poverty thinking and a sign that you do not trust the angels to meet all your needs. Everything we need will always be provided.

They also say we must not accumulate too many things, because they do not really belong to us. Just like we cannot be possessed, things should not be possessed either. It is wrong to call things "possessions." Everything in life is energy, and energy needs to flow.

The angels recommend that we declutter our lives and get rid of the excess. We must give away all the clothes we no longer wear and the books we will never reread, and recycle or give away our old papers and all the useless things that adorn the corners of our home. Getting rid of all that clutter will increase the flow of energy around us, and abundance will flow into our lives more easily.

Gratitude

The angels say that to attract abundance, it is so important to be grateful. Giving thanks for the abundance you already have in your life will ensure that more will follow. We all have something to be grateful for. I'm sure that if you stop to look around, you will realize how much you already have. Do you have a roof over your head? Do you have enough to eat and clothes to wear? Maybe even an education? Then you are already rich. Take time every day to be grateful for what you have and you will be rewarded with so much more.

Generosity

The angels remind us of how important it is to be generous and to share what we have. Often we feel nudged to give something to someone and we do not do it. We are attached to our material things and are afraid to let them go. We hang on to our money for dear life, afraid that we won't receive any more.

I remember the time my brother was moving out west and he had very little means. It was a hard time for him. I picked him up at the airport and he stayed with me overnight. The next day, I went to the ATM and gave him forty dollars. I myself did not have a lot of means at the time either. The money actually came from my credit account. The very next day, I received an Easter card from my grandmother with forty dollars in it. I understood at that moment that the angels were teaching me an important lesson: when we give, we receive. When we give graciously with our heart, even when we don't have much, it is like saying to the angels, "I trust that you are caring and providing for me," and they will.

The other day, I saw a video by Tony Robbins where he tells the story about when he learned about financial flow. He was down to his last dollars and decided to go to a buffet. After paying his bill, he only had enough money to come back for one more meal. A nicely dressed young boy came in with his mother. The young man opened the door for his mother and pulled out her chair. Tony was so moved by the genteel qualities of this young man that he gave him his last dollars to pay for his "date" with his mom. He left the restaurant not knowing where his next meal was going to come from. He arrived home to find a large check from a friend who had owed him money. At that moment, he understood the principle of flow and faith.

Follow the nudging of your heart to give. Give graciously without expecting anything in return. When someone gives to you, pay it forward to someone else. Never expect the person to whom you give to return the favor. Know that the angels will bring you what you need, when you need it. Keep the faith.

The angels also encourage us to be generous with our time, energy, ideas, opportunities, contacts, and knowledge. Always look for ways that you can better help and serve others. Be ready to lend a helping hand and share your ideas with others, if it can help them in some way. If someone needs a contact that might help them out, be generous and share your contacts. Remember that what goes around comes around. Too many people are afraid of competition these days and are afraid to share their knowledge. Remember that the more you give, the more you receive. Why not help someone climb the ladder of life? Remember that one day, you may need help climbing up too.

Finally, the angels tell us to stop hoarding our money. We are so afraid of lacking money that we do not allow ourselves to spend. We are invited to be generous with ourselves and with our money. If you feel guided to give to someone, give generously and with a good heart. If you *feel* guided to purchase something, buy all means buy it. This is not the same as impulse buying. Impulse buying is thinking, "I might wear this next winter," while inspired buying is feeling, "Aw! What a beautiful and perfect dress!" You feel the longing in your heart, and then you think, "I don't know where I would wear that!" or "Do I really need that?" That is your ego speaking. Do you see the difference? Impulse buying is the ego convincing you to buy something you don't need, and inspired buying is your angels guiding you through your heart to recognize what is meant for you and then your ego will try to convince you not to buy it.

When we feel the "Aw!" it is a recognition that something is for us. I've noticed in my own life that when I don't make that purchase, I always regret it. When we talk ourselves out of a purchase, it is usually to "save" money. The angels say that is poverty thinking, especially when we have the money and can afford it.

So follow the guidance in your heart to be generous with yourself and others. Have faith and know that when you give, you receive even when you give to yourself.

Prayer for Manifesting Abundance

Here is a sample prayer that you can use to manifest more abundance in your life.

Worthiness

"Lord God, I am worthy of your goodness, your grace, and your blessings. By the simple fact that I exist, I am worthy of abundance. I free myself from all negative emotions and false beliefs about abundance that do not serve me. I know my will is your will and you only want what is in my highest good."

Desire

"Dearest angels, what I desire most in life and what would really make me happy is more time, money, energy, ideas, and opportunities to do the things that stir my heart. I deeply desire to achieve the dreams that you have put in my heart."

Trust

"My dearest angels, I ask you to bring me an abundance of resources, including creativity, freedom, and vitality. Lord God and my dearest angels, I trust you completely. I know you have heard my request and you are already working on its fulfillment. I promise you, my dearest angels, that I will follow your divine guidance."

Imagination

I reserve at least ten minutes a day to imagine that I have all the resources I need. I pretend I already have them.

Gratitude

"Thank you in advance, Lord God and my dearest angels, for the fulfillment of my greatest desire for more time, money, energy, ideas, and opportunities. Thank you for the creativity, the freedom, the vitality, the well-being, the gifts, and the blessings. Thank you, thank you, thank you."

Manifesting Financial Abundance

Many of us desire to have more financial abundance in our lives. Know that financial abundance alone will not make you happy. Relationships and a sense of purpose are what makes most of us truly happy.

Back in Ontario, I had a great career in the government. I had a high-level position, was very well paid, and had excellent work conditions and benefits. I had all the material things I believed should make me happy, but I wasn't. I prayed to the angels to bring me what I needed to feel happy. The following day, I met my lovely neighbor Dorinda (whose name means "gift from God"), who taught me about Reiki and introduced me to a wonderful group of native ladies. That is where I found my true happiness, through new friends, new discoveries, and a new sense of purpose to my life.

We all need balance in our lives, and we may at some point want to know how to attract more financial abundance. In my private consultations, the angels have given my clients lots of very practical advice on the subject, so I would like to share this information with you.

Beliefs

First, the angels say the main reason we lack financial flow is because of our fears and negative beliefs about money. We have to stop being afraid of lacking money, of not having enough, because we attract what we fear. If you live with a knot in your stomach because you are afraid of not being able to pay your bills, that is exactly what you will attract in your life. Many of us were raised by parents who were afraid of not having enough money, and they passed those fears on to us. Many of us have heard, "Money doesn't grow on trees!" or "Money doesn't make you happy!"

Those kinds of thoughts are based on the belief of lack. I believe that money comes from God and an abundant universe. The angels remind us that God is our source of abundance, not our employer or anyone else. I have received money in ways I could never have imagined, but for God and the angels, miracles are their specialty.

Money *can* bring happiness, especially if you use the money to fulfill your life's purpose, to serve others or make them happy, or to realize a dream that is dear to your heart.

Have you ever wondered, "What if my parents' beliefs were false?" Have you ever stopped to ask yourself what your beliefs are about money and if these beliefs are serving you?

You can change your ideas about money by using positive affirmations, such as these:

- Financial abundance is my birthright!
- I deserve abundance!
- I deserve to be financially free!
- I am blessed with abundance!
- I am worthy of God's goodness!
- I graciously accept the constant stream of blessings reserved for me!
- I graciously accept the best in my life now!
- I am financially secure!
- I am supported fully today and every day of my life!

The angels remind us of how important it is to have the conviction that they only want what is best for us, and it is equally important to believe in abundance. In fact, financial freedom and abundance are our birthright. One of the biggest reasons we do not have financial abundance and all that we want in our life is because we do not feel worthy of it. Know that you are as worthy of financial success as you are of being alive. You just need to believe!

Debt

"What if I am in debt over my head?" you ask me. The angels recommend focusing on paying down your debt and reducing your expenses. When you receive your bills, do not panic; instead, be grateful to your creditors for trusting you and believing in your ability to pay. Ask the angels to provide you what you need, and trust that money will follow. Have absolute faith in their ability to provide for you. Thank your angels in advance for their help.

Prayer to Settle Debt

"My dearest angels, thank you for your assistance in paying my debts. I know that God alone is the true source of my abundance. I ask you, dearest angels, to help me pay my debts and to free me from all negative beliefs about money.

"I am grateful for all of the abundance that I have in my life. I remain open to any divine guidance that will bring me the right people and the right opportunities at the right time, and I promise you, my dearest angels, that I will follow your divine guidance to free myself of debt.

"Thank you in advance for your kindness, your grace, and your blessings toward me as well as others.

"Amen."

Compensating

Sometimes we compensate by buying things we do not need to fill a void. We tell ourselves, "If I have to stay in this job that I no longer love but that pays the bills, I may as well give myself a little luxury!" This is called compensation. When we are unhappy, we compensate to fill the emptiness inside. Some people fill the void with food, others with sex, drugs, or alcohol, and some of us shop. We each have our own way of compensating for our unhappiness.

Most of us have compensated for our unhappiness at some point in our lives. But soon thereafter, we realized that impulse purchases bring us only fleeting happiness. We must stop and ask ourselves, "What do I really need to be happy?" Most of us would be surprised to know that what we need is not necessarily more material things but rather for our life to have more meaning.

Pray to the angels: "Thank you, my dearest angels, for helping me release any need to compensate for my unhappiness. Help me know what it is that I truly need to be happy, and give me the courage to make positive and healthy changes in order to create and experience more joy and a more fulfilling life."

Increasing Your Cash Flow

Here are some tips from the angels about increasing your cash flow.

USE CASH

Paper does not have the same energy as plastic. Plastic disconnects you from your money. It is important to feel the essence of paper money. The angels suggest that when you pay with paper money, rub the dollars bills between your fingers and say, "Thank you! Thank you! Thank you! Keep it coming!"

USE FENG SHUI

Feng shui is an ancient Chinese art of decorating to attract good energy in our home or work environment. To attract more money in your life, place a container in the wealth and abundance sector of your home, which is the far left corner of your house based on the front door. Fill the container with money to save for something really special, like a special vacation or a new piece of furniture. You should not make yourself miserable in the process of paying off your debts either. You must love paying your bills while anticipating something pleasant in the future.

SPEND WISELY

When it come to making purchases, it is important to spend wisely. It is okay to have material things if you can afford them. We all deserve nice things, but we should not go into debt to have them.

ALLOW MONEY TO FLOW

Allow your money to flow. Do not hoard in fear of not receiving any more. There have been times in my life when I felt guided to make a certain purchase and didn't out of fear. Like when I saw a beautiful crystal ball in a store. My heart leaped when I saw it, and it spoke to me when I held it in my hands. I had the money to buy it, but I was afraid of spending it. When I finally decided to get the crystal ball, it was too late. Months later, I realized that I didn't have more money because I hadn't bought it. I probably had less money because of my fear and hoarding and not allowing the money to flow.

We have to allow money to flow in our lives and trust that the angels will bring us more. If we don't spend the cash we have on what I call "investments" (such as tools, books, conferences, workshops, and even clothes) that the angels guide us to buy, we can be almost guaranteed that they will get us to spend our money by sending us an unexpected bill for an expense of the same value. Know that the angels are helping us build our faith in them and in the flow of financial abundance.

Manifesting Money

I believe that the need to manifest money is rare. Money is often a means to an end. For example, let's say you want to take a trip, start a business, buy a house, etc. Money can be a way to help you achieve those dreams, but it is not the only way. In fact, you need money to pay debts, and even then there is the possibility that your debts might be forgiven. So how you formulate your request to the angels is very important. What do you really want or need? How will this money you think you need serve you? Ask for that and not for the money itself. Let the angels surprise you with their imaginative ways of answering your prayers.

A friend of mine was renting a cottage that was pretty run-down. She really wanted it to be renovated, but the owner had no plans to invest money. I suggested she pray to the angels, not for the money but for help improving her living space. The very next week there was a storm and water leaked into the cottage, causing a relative amount of damage. They had to redo the walls and floors, which was exactly what she had wanted. The bonus was that the insurance company paid for it. The owner only had to pay the deduction.

Back in 2009, I had planned a trip to go to the "I Can Do It!" conference in San Diego, California, organized by Hay House. One day I got an email announcing a conference by Neale Donald Walsch, author of the famous Conversations with God series of books. Mr. Walsch is one of my favorite authors. The angels had asked me in 2004 if I would like to meet him one day. After so many years, I had completely forgotten about it. I had not paid too much attention to the email about his conference, but in the days that followed, the idea of meeting Mr. Walsch often came back to me. So through an Internet search I saw that he was giving a conference in San Francisco the weekend before I was to attend the one in San Diego. I told my angels, "I feel that you want me to meet Mr. Walsch. If this is what you want, then you will have to bring me more money." It was going to cost me much more to stay in California for ten days.

The next day at the office, there was a big brown envelope with the word "confidential" on it in my mailbox. The envelope contained a letter from the pay office, and it said that they had forgotten to stop my payment for the arrears of my pension fund. They included a check for the $1,500 they owed me for this error. For me, it was a gift from the angels—a confirmation of my plans and the money I needed to stay in San Francisco. I could never have imagined receiving money in this way. So now, when I need money, I simply pray to the angels and I know that they will find a way, even if I can't see it yet.

If you desperately need money, you can pray to your angels: "My dearest angels, you know the state of my financial situation. I pray to you for help. Thank you for creating a financial miracle in my life right now and for bringing me the money I need."

Last fall I prayed this very prayer. Thirty minutes later, I received a message from a lady who canceled my biggest event for the fall. I couldn't believe it! But I said to the angels, "I trust that you know what you are doing. Thank you for taking care of my financial situation." I trusted and I let it go. A few days later, I got another invitation to do an event that required much less preparation, and I ended up making three times the money.

Trust, trust, trust. Know that you are immensely loved and not alone. Have faith that God and the angels are looking out for you. They are just waiting for the opportunity to prove it to you!

Prayer for Manifesting Money

Here is a sample prayer that you can use to manifest more cash flow in your life.

Worthiness

"Lord God, I am worthy of your goodness, your grace, and your blessings. By the simple fact that I exist, I am worthy of money and prosperity. I free myself from all negative emotions and false beliefs about money that no longer serve me. I know that my will is your will and you only want what is best for me."

Desire

"Dearest angels, I desire to be financially free. I desire to be free of debt, have enough income to cover all my basic expenses, and have ample money left over to pay for some luxuries."

Trust

"Lord God and dearest angels, I trust you completely. I know you have heard my request and you are already working on its fulfillment. I promise you, my dearest angels, that I will follow your divine guidance, including being generous with my money."

Imagination

I reserve at least ten minutes a day to imagine that I am already financially free, that I have money and prosperity in my life, and I pretend I already have it. I feel the joy and confidence that this financial freedom brings.

Gratitude

"I am truly grateful for my material and financial blessings. Thank you in advance, Lord God and my dearest angels, for financial freedom, prosperity, and abundance. Thank you for the fulfillment of my greatest desire to be free of any debt and to have more than enough income to cover all my basic needs and ample money left over to pay for some luxuries. Thank you, thank you, thank you."

EXERCISE
Manifesting Abundance

The angels say the best way to manifest more abundance in your life is to respect and honor what you have already, to be grateful and share it with others.

Abundance is not only money but also time, energy, ideas, and opportunities.

For each of these categories, write down how you can better respect, honor, show gratitude for, and share what you already have. Here are some examples:

Time

+ "I choose to spend one hour a day learning to play a musical instrument."
+ "I choose to spend one hour a week doing charity work."

Energy

+ "I choose to walk for thirty minutes a day."
+ "I choose to meditate for twenty minutes a day."

Ideas

+ "I research the idea of starting my own business."

Opportunities

+ "I choose to accept the invitation to do public speaking."

Money

+ "I choose to be more generous with my money."
+ "I choose to purchase a nice purse with my money."

Worthiness

You know by now that worthiness plays a big part in any manifestation of what we want. Let's look at this subject with regard to abundance.

Write down your beliefs about abundance (time, energy, ideas, opportunities, and money). For example:

- "I can't have it all."
- "There is never enough time."
- "Twenty-four hours in a day is just not enough."

For each of your beliefs, ask yourself if this belief serves to attract abundance or repel it.

Then rewrite each belief and say you are ready to release it:

- "I release the belief that I cannot have it all."
- "I release the belief that there is never enough time."
- "I release the belief that twenty-four hours in a day is not enough."

Now create new beliefs, such as these:

- "I have all the time I need."
- "I have everything I need and more."
- "I have enough."

Desire

Ask yourself, "What do I really desire in my heart to be happy?" For example:

+ "I desire more time to enjoy the things that stir my heart, such as writing, meditating, walking, and meeting new clients."
+ "I desire energy and vitality to achieve the dreams that are dear to my soul."

Trust

Open your arms wide to receive the abundance of the universe. Notice the messages from your angels that guide you to better manage what you already have, make time for you, set boundaries, rest, take action, etc. Take note of the actions you feel guided to follow regarding the abundance of time, energy, money, etc.

Imagination

Describe your dream life in which you have plenty of time, energy, money, ideas, opportunities, and whatever else you feel you need.

Gratitude

Write down whatever makes you feel grateful. For example:

+ "I am grateful for my creativity, my well-being, and all of my gifts."
+ "I am so truly grateful for all the time I need to work on the projects that are dear to my heart, all while maintaining a balanced life."

EXERCISE
Manifesting Money

The angels say the need to manifest money is rare. Money is often a means to an end. For example, let's say you want to take a trip, start a business, buy a house, etc. How you formulate your request to the angels is very important. What do you really want? How will this money you think you need serve you? Ask for that and not for the money itself. Let the angels surprise you with the imaginative ways they can answer your prayers.

Worthiness

Start by writing down your beliefs about money. Here are some examples:

+ "Money doesn't fall from the sky."
+ "There is never enough money."
+ "Money goes out faster than it comes in."

For each of your beliefs, ask yourself if it is helping you attract money or repelling it.

Then rewrite each belief and state that you are ready to release it. For example:

+ "I release the belief that money does not fall from the sky."
+ "I release the belief that there is never enough money."
+ "I release the belief that money goes out faster than it comes in."

Now create new beliefs in the present tense. For example:

+ "Money does come from the sky; it is from God!"
+ "I always have more than enough money."

+ "I allow money to flow freely so that it returns to me faster and more abundantly."

+ "I am able to pay for all my basic needs and have ample money left over to buy myself the occasional luxury."

Desire

Ask yourself, "What do I really need financially to be happy? What do I truly desire in life?" Here is an example:

+ "I would like to be free of debt, have enough income to cover all my basic expenses, and have ample money left over to pay for the occasional luxury."

Trust

Open your arms wide to receive money from God and the angels. Take note of any actions you feel guided to follow regarding money and prosperity.

Imagination

Describe what you will do with this money.

Gratitude

Write down everything for which you are grateful. Here are some examples:

+ "I am thankful that I am able to take care of all of my basic financial and material needs and for always having more than enough."

+ "I am so truly grateful that you've always provided so generously for me."

13
MANIFESTING OUR
LIFE'S PURPOSE

"Don't die with your music still in you."
—*Wayne Dyer*

The angels say that we can manifest all the material things and financial abundance we want, but if our life has no meaning, we will not be truly happy and fulfilled. We must start by discovering and manifesting our life's purpose and then all the material things will ensue. In Matthew 6:33, Jesus said, "Seek first the kingdom of God, and his righteousness, and all these things shall be added unto you."

The kingdom of God, or heaven, is not some place we go to after we die but is really a state of oneness with the divine that we can experience while we are here on earth. It is within us. It is a state of peace, love, and well-being that comes from living the life our soul desires. It is up to each and every one of us to find this place of oneness, of peace with a higher power within ourselves, to find our true essence and purpose. When we live constantly connected to this divine power and to who we really are, and we are living a purposeful life, we can achieve great things. With the help of our divine friends, the angels, through their love and grace, we can manifest an amazing life.

We all ask ourselves the same questions: "Why am I here?" "What is the purpose of my life?" "What is my reason for being?" Many people feel that their lives are devoid of meaning and that they do not matter. Even if they have a good job that affords them a gorgeous home, a beautiful car, exotic vacations, and luxuries from time to time, they still feel that there is something lacking in their lives. They work forty hours a week or more in a job they do not like and they cannot wait for the weekend. They work all their lives waiting for retirement to realize a few dreams. They spend most of their lives on hold instead of living their lives today. They are always looking forward to something in the future and do not take advantage of this moment, or they are at the end of their lives and have regrets. More often than not, they regret not having lived their passion.

We often hear about people dying just before their retirement or soon after taking it. They waited all their lives to live what they really wanted to live, to realize their dreams, but these people were trapped in the system. They bought into the idea of devoting their lives to a company or to public service, with the promise of a beautiful retirement later. "Work for us and we promise to take care of you later. You can enjoy your freedom when you retire." Back then, they talked about "Freedom 55." Today, there is talk of "Freedom 67" for the next generation, and some may not experience the freedom at all. I believe that this new young generation will not be trapped. They saw their parents or grandparents sacrifice their lives for companies that quickly replaced and forgot them, or for a government that dropped them during budget cuts.

We all have a dream in our heart that we would like to accomplish. We all have a passion for something we dream of living. But often, reason takes over and our beliefs and fears limit us. We are afraid.

We do not want to be pretentious and believe that we are capable of something "special" or "greater." Our ego plays tricks on us. Even the words of our parents and friends play in our heads: "But you have to earn a living!" "Be realistic!" "You cannot leave a job in the public service!" "How will you prepare for your retirement?" "Are you sure you can live on your passion alone?" These phrases are meant to make us doubt ourselves and keep us frozen in fear, and then we end up asking ourselves, "What if they are right?" Remember that well-intentioned people will project their own fears onto you.

More and more people realize that life is meant for living today, in this moment. Life is meant for being and not for having. For if we live in hopes of always having something and that something is in the future, that means that our happiness is always dependent on what we will have in the future. It is important to *be* happy and to *be* alive today, and for our life to have meaning and a sense of purpose.

God has put a dream in each one of our hearts. He has given us talents, gifts, and abilities specific to each one of us in order to realize our life's purpose. He has given us experiences, trials, and challenges to prepare us for our destiny. He has even lit the flame in our hearts that we call passion, to propel us toward our future. He shows us signs all along the way leading us to our dreams. Know that we have everything we need to reach them.

The angels tell me that the only thing that is really important in life is to be happy, to be fully alive and present in this moment—not just on weekends or when we retire, but in every moment of every day. And the surest way to be happy and joyful in every moment and to give meaning to our lives is to do what excites us, what makes us feel alive, and what brings us joy.

The angels also remind us that life is also about giving to others. Life is not about merely surviving or about accumulating material goods; it is really about giving to others, whether it be a smile, a prayer, or a helping hand. Have you noticed that when you smile at people, you feel happier? What you give to others comes back to you. Try it. You will see that even on a day when you feel moody or melancholy, when you give a beautiful smile to someone, you will feel better. Life is about giving to others.

What made me realize that it was time for me to pursue my passion for writing was a song on the radio. One day I heard a song that spoke to my heart, and it came to me that I would never have heard that song if the artist had allowed herself to be influenced by negativity, such as "You cannot live off your music!" "Artists starve!" Furthermore, I realized that just as the artist had inspired me through her song, maybe it was possible that I might inspire someone through my book. Even if I inspired just one person, it would be worth the joy I had in writing it.

One evening, I heard a person on television list three things a person needs to be happy in life: a job you love, a reason for being, and a person with whom to share your happiness.

It's important to have balance in our lives. A simple job cannot fill every need, and love alone cannot fill the void that is in our soul if we do not fulfill our life's purpose. When I was young, I felt I was going to do something important in my life and that I would be somebody. In my early twenties, I felt I was going to write a book on the subject of grace, which for me means "God's presence." I had a deep desire to share my personal experiences of how God and the angels are present in our lives and how recognizing this is simply a matter of perception.

I believe that God and the angels are present in all of our lives, whether a person believes or not. There is a universal force present in our lives guiding us, protecting us, and leading us in the right direction to assist us in achieving our life's purpose and God's great plan.

From childhood, we all carry a dream in our hearts. The most important thing in our lives is to discover and realize this dream.

It is our responsibility to discover and fulfill our life's purpose. Each of us has something special to share with others, and like our beloved Wayne Dyer said, "Don't die with your music still in you."

Deep down, we all know what makes our heart sing, but we do not listen. We think, "But it cannot be! I am not that special!" Too often we ignore what God has planned for us because we do not feel worthy of doing what our soul really wants us to do in life. We are afraid of what people will think, we are afraid to fail, and sometimes we are afraid to succeed. We think, "And what if it doesn't work? How will I pay my bills?" We all ask ourselves the same questions.

But in our hearts, we all know what we really want in life. My clients always tell me at the end of a consultation, "I knew it, but I just couldn't believe it!"

It's not easy to listen to our inner voice. It takes courage to do what our heart really wants us to do. I also believe that our guides and angels are constantly trying to remind us of our life's purpose, but to recognize it, we have to be still, listen to our heart, and pay attention to the signs.

To discover your passion, the angels suggest you ask yourself the following: "If there was no job security and no guarantee that I would keep this position until I retire, is there something else that would interest me more? What is keeping me here? What would my soul prefer to do? If money or time was no object, what would I really like to do with my life? What would make my heart sing?"

Is it possible that the job cuts in your company are one strategy the angels use to push you toward a new job or career that would make you happier? Remember that life is always on your side; it is working for you and not against you. Changes are always for the better, so don't be afraid. Trust that God and the angels know the desires of your heart and what is best for you.

The signs are always there. The angels are constantly speaking to us if we would just listen. They usually lead us forward one small step at a time. We do not always see the entire stairwell, but we must take it one step at a time and trust where we are being led. Life is like traveling on the road. We have a final destination, but we do not see the whole journey at a glance. There are mountains and valleys, curves, fog, and road signs. We must trust that the signs are leading us in the right direction. We must not disregard any of the signs, because we may get lost. It is the same thing in our lives.

What stirs your passion? The arts? Children? Elderly people? Teaching? Construction? Writing? Antiques?

Remember that your life's purpose is not necessarily connected to your job.

I have met people for whom their life's purpose was to care for their community through prayer, and for others it was through politics. Many women are here on earth to care for the indigo children or to be the mother of all the children in their neighborhood.

There are other people who are simply here to learn how to have fun. I met a woman who liked to sing and enjoyed Irish music, but her husband did not support her. Her need to sing was vital for her, so she started taking singing lessons. Her evenings fulfilled her as she enjoyed singing for the elderly.

Our life's purpose is as unique for each of us as our fingerprints. For example, there are many writers in the world and many have a similar message, but they each have a particular style that will attract the people who need to receive their message and in a way that will resonate with them. It is the same in all areas. There is no competition. The people we are meant to serve will naturally be attracted to us.

How do you identify your life's purpose? The first hint is that it will serve others. That is your main motivation. Your life's purpose is always a call to serve others.

What interests you? What dream do you have in your heart that you have not yet realized and would like to share with the world?

What gifts, qualities, or talents do you have that could be of service to the people around you? Maybe you have the ability to communicate, to paint, to cook, to put people at ease, or to counsel.

Ask your angels to show you your qualities, talents, and gifts. Everyone has something special and unique to them.

Say, "Thank you, my darling angels, for helping me see my special talents and gifts, and thank you for helping me discover my life's purpose."

I have noticed the divine signs all my life. When I was fourteen, I used to read tarot cards for my girlfriends. At eighteen, I did a secretarial course where I learned to type. At twenty, I had the feeling I was going to write a book someday. I was guided to go to university when I was twenty-four years old, and that is where I had my first encounter with a spirit and discovered my passion for writing.

At the age of twenty-eight, my friends encouraged me to have a fortune-telling booth at a festival. This really required me to step outside of my comfort zone. But that experience proved unforgettable for me! Strangely, I truly felt in my element. At thirty-five, I was guided toward an Angel Therapy™ class with Doreen Virtue, where all my clairs really opened up, and from there I was asked to teach. Then the angels inspired me to begin writing my first manuscript. Since then, I have been giving angelic and mediumship readings, conferences, and workshops, and I still write regularly. I left my government job to do this work full-time. I listen to the loving guidance of my angels and I follow the signs. I feel that my soul is happy with my progress.

When I do not follow their guidance, I become depressed, anxious, or exhausted.

And so, a second hint that guides you toward your life's purpose is your level of wellbeing. If what you are doing is making you feel exhausted, depressed, or sick, it is not for you. But if you feel happy and alive, you are on the right track. It is that simple. When people say "Follow your heart," what they really mean is follow what makes you happy and joyful in your heart.

When you feel guided in a certain direction and the signs are clear, trust that everything will be provided for you. Maybe money may not be plentiful right now, but trust. Proceed if you feel guided to do so, and everything will be provided. We can't always wait for the conditions to be perfect to move forward with our life; we have to trust that what we need will be provided. The important thing is to listen to the guidance of your angels, move forward, and trust. Sometimes moving into the unknown requires a great leap of faith. Know that you are not alone.

Honoring God and the angels by being all that you are meant to be is the greatest proof of faith and love in yourself and in them. Following your passion and fulfilling your life's purpose is the greatest gift you can give yourself and others. You are special, you are unique, and you have something magnificent to share with others that nobody else can do in your place! Go forth in faith!

Prayer for Manifesting Your Life's Purpose

To manifest your life's purpose, you can say this prayer daily.

Worthiness

"Lord God, I am worthy of your goodness, your grace, and your blessings. I know I am special and I have something unique to share with others. I believe I can make a living from my passion. I know that you have placed a special dream in my heart that I alone can achieve. You have given me all the talents, skills, gifts, and experiences I need to realize my full potential and be all that I am meant to be. I know that my will is your will and you only want what is best for me."

Desire

"Dearest angels, I wish to honor you by realizing my passion, my life's purpose, and by being all that I am meant to be. I ask you, my dearest angels, to show me the way, to guide me toward my passion so I can build on my gifts, qualities, and skills for the greater good of all."

Trust

"My dearest angels, I trust you completely. I know you have heard my request and are already working on its fulfillment. I may not know the road to follow or how things will all work out, but I promise you, my dearest angels, that I will follow your divine guidance. I will trust and follow all the signs you put on my path."

Imagination

I reserve at least ten minutes a day to imagine myself realizing my passion, my biggest dreams. I imagine that I am already living it. I feel the joy, love, and wholeness that this new life brings.

Gratitude

"Thank you in advance, Lord God and my dearest angels, for helping me with my confidence in myself and in my abilities. Thank you for giving me the courage to follow your guidance and fulfill my biggest dreams. I am so truly grateful for the gifts you have given me and for this wonderful life's purpose! Thank you for the passion that suits me so perfectly! Thank you, thank you, thank you."

EXERCISE
Manifesting Your Life's Purpose

This exercise will help you take a good look at your life to find what makes your heart sing.

Remember that you are special, you are unique, and you have something magnificent to share with others that nobody else can do in your place!

Worthiness

Write down any negative beliefs you have about your life's purpose. Here are some examples:

- "I am not special."
- "I have no gifts to share with others."
- "I cannot make a living from my passion."

For each of your beliefs, ask yourself if this belief is helping you achieve your life's purpose or not.

Then rewrite each negative belief and state that you are ready to release it. For example:

- "I release the belief that I am not special."
- "I release the belief that I have no gifts to share with others."
- "I release the belief that I cannot make a living from my passion."

Now create new beliefs:

+ "I am special."
+ "I have something unique to share with others."
+ "I can make a living from my passion."

Desire

What are your interests? What dreams do you have in your heart that you have not yet fulfilled? Here is an example:

+ "I would like to share God and the angels' loving message with the world."

What gifts, qualities, or talents do you have that could be of service to the people around you? Maybe you have the ability to communicate, to paint, to cook, to put people at ease, or to counsel. Write them down now.

+ "I have a gift for communicating with angels and deceased loved ones, counseling others, writing, and speaking."

Ask your angels to show you your qualities, talents, and gifts. Everyone has something special and unique to them.

+ "I am humble, authentic, compassionate, empathetic, and considerate. I have a gift for communicating, writing, counseling, and speaking. I have the gift of mediumship."

Ask yourself the following questions: "If there was no job security and no guarantee that I would keep this position until I retire, is there something else that would interest me more? What is keeping me here? What would my soul prefer to do? If money or time was no object, what would I really

like to do with my life? What would make my heart sing?"
For example:

- "I really would like to connect people with their angels, guides, God, and their deceased loved ones during private consultations and in workshops. I would like to share with others my knowledge through books and speaking engagements."

Trust

Stay open to all messages you receive regarding your life's purpose. Are there new opportunities available to you? Ask your angels to guide you and follow the divine signs.

Imagination

Imagine yourself already living your passion. How would you spend your days? Describe your perfect day living your passion, your life's purpose.

Gratitude

Write down what makes you grateful. For example:

- "I am grateful for the gifts God has given me!"
- "I am grateful to have such a wonderful life's purpose!"
- "I am grateful for this passion that suits me perfectly!"

14
FEAR

"There is only one thing that makes a dream impossible
to achieve: the fear of failure."
—*Paulo Coelho*

Toward the end of writing this book, I woke up one morning with the revelation that there was a common thread in all of the chapters on manifesting with the angels. Each chapter always came to the same conclusion. Only one thing keeps us from living our lives fully. One emotion deprives us of living a healthy, happy, abundant life while being in love and realizing our life's purpose. One emotion has kept us sick, unhappy, poor, and feeling unloved and without direction for thousands of years. It has affected entire generations. This emotion is *fear*.

We basically all have the same desire to be happy. We strive our whole lives to stay healthy, in shape, find love, build a family, and earn money, all while doing work that pleases us and prepares us for retirement. We all live in a state of survival.

For many people, there is always something wrong. They are either sick, out of shape, unhappy in their work, in a loveless marriage, or living under the poverty line.

After several years of reflection on my own life, trying to understand why I was sick, unhappy, loveless, and staying in a job I no longer enjoyed, the angels told me one morning that one thing was keeping me from living my life fully: fear.

Different Fears

That same day when the angels whispered this idea to me in my ear, I noticed my own string of fear-based thoughts: "I should eat fruit for breakfast. Eating too much white bread is not good for my health, and especially with cheese spread. It must not be good for my body because it is not natural. I have not slept enough. I am going to be tired today."

This dialogue that was running through my mind shows that I was afraid to eat bread and cheese spread. I was afraid for my health. I was also afraid of not getting enough sleep and of being tired. All these fears ran though my head in just ten seconds.

We attract what we fear, so imagine what I was creating that morning.

Here is a list of common fears:

Health

+ Fear of overeating
+ Fear of eating too much sugar, meat, or bread
+ Fear of not eating enough vegetables and fruits
+ Fear of smoking too much or of not being able to stop
+ Fear of drinking too much alcohol or of becoming or being an alcoholic
+ Fear of having slept too much or not enough
+ Fear of being too hot, too cold, or tired

- Fear of getting sick or becoming disabled or dependent
- Fear of depression

Appearance

- Fear of putting on weight
- Fear of losing weight
- Fear of being too beautiful
- Fear of being too ugly
- Fear of not being fit enough
- Fear of being too muscular
- Fear of not being physically perfect
- Fear of not being attractive

Love

- Fear of not finding love
- Fear of not being lovable
- Fear of not being loved
- Fear of not being respected
- Fear of losing ourselves in love
- Fear of allowing ourselves to be loved
- Fear of surrendering and being vulnerable
- Fear of not making the right choice in love

At Work

- Fear of standing our ground or making bad decisions
- Fear of not being smart, fast, efficient, or profitable enough
- Fear of failing exams or competitions or of not living up to the expectations of others and our own

+ Fear of disappointing our boss, our colleagues, and our clients

Money

+ Fear of not having enough money
+ Fear of not being able to pay our bills or take care of our family
+ Fear of not saving enough for a decent retirement
+ Fear of bankruptcy
+ Fear of being ripped off when buying goods and services

Life in General

+ Fear of being rejected, abandoned, humiliated, or betrayed
+ Fear of experiencing injustice
+ Fear of failure or success
+ Fear of displeasing others or not measuring up
+ Fear of traveling
+ Fear of dreaming or daring to take a chance or risk
+ Fear of moving forward, standing our ground, or being all that God intended for us to be
+ Fear of the future
+ Fear of living
+ Fear of dying

Do you see yourself in these fears? I have noticed how often I feel afraid in one single day and just how much my fears have been blocking me. My fears have sometimes stopped my momentum dead in its tracks and prevented me from living the beautiful life God and the angels have intended for me. In 2009, I felt guided to leave my job to pursue my spiritual career full-time, but I was too afraid to leave. I had a hundred clients on a waiting list but was afraid that I wouldn't be able to make it financially. I was paralyzed by fear and my lack of faith.

The Origin of Fear

When we were babies, we were not afraid of anything. Babies have an intuition, a sensitivity, that protects them. If they sense something is wrong, they will cry and let you know.

Over the years, children are influenced by parents and caregivers. They imitate them. For example, if the parent or sitter is nervous, the child will feel it and become nervous too. If the mother is afraid of spiders, chances are the child will develop this fear too. Parents instill fear in their children from birth. They will say things like, "Be nice!" "You're not nice!" or "You're a bad boy!" Children then develop a fear of losing love.

Next we hear, "Don't run too fast!" "Be careful crossing the street!" "Don't talk to strangers!" "Don't eat too fast!" "You're going to fall!" These words are always well intentioned and are meant to protect the child, but they instill fear as well. Over the years, the words become, "Money doesn't grow on trees!" "You have to work hard!" "You have to have a respectable job!" We then develop fears of taking risks, of daring, or of following our dreams. We begin to lack confidence in ourselves and we lack faith in life. When we are afraid of the future, it simply means we do not trust in God and the angels to take care of us. When we are afraid of losing the love of our family, we do not trust them either.

The angels invite us to look at what is blocking us, what it is we fear. When we look at it and see it for what it is, we can transform it. We cannot change what we do not acknowledge.

So look at what is wrong in your life and ask yourself, "What am I afraid of? Where does this fear come from? Is it justified? Is it serving me?"

Take a look at your life to see where fear may be stopping you or holding you back, and see what solutions you might find to overcome your fears and finally live the life of your dreams.

Most people are afraid of change. They are afraid to change jobs, leave their spouse, disappoint their family, or follow their dreams. How can you let go of these fears? You have to look past the fear. The angels invite you to go into your imagination and ask yourself, "What is the worst thing that could happen?"

Perhaps you risk losing your job, or your spouse, or all your money. And then what? Imagine yourself in the worst possible situation and see how you would handle it. There is always a solution to everything. It may be different from what you would like, but it exists. Maybe you will make less money than before, but you may also be happier too. Perhaps you will live alone for a while, but you will meet someone new eventually. Maybe your home will be smaller, but you will be happy anyway. There is always a solution, an answer to every problem. Also remember that you are not alone. You are surrounded by your loving angels who are just waiting to assist you on your path. Remember to call on them in difficult times when you are afraid and need reassurance.

If we are living in fear, we need to build our faith. We need to believe that God and the angels are caring for us. We need to remember that we are never alone. We are all one. We are all connected to each other and to the divine. God and the angels are part of us and we are part of them. They want what we want. It cannot be otherwise. But we must move forward fearlessly, hand in hand with them.

The angels also want you to trust in your ability to overcome adversity and to figure things out. Believe in yourself. Know that you have everything inside of you to succeed. Have complete faith and confidence in yourself. Believe in yourself and in your future. Stay positive and keep focused on the benefits of making positive changes in your life. Always stay focused on what you can gain rather than what you may lose.

My motto for change has always been "I am more afraid to be stuck in yesterday than I am of tomorrow." I know what yesterday entailed and I have always believed that tomorrow is full of possibilities. Keeping that in mind has always helped me move forward more fearlessly.

So when we experience fear, the angels recommend that we focus on what we want and not on what we don't want. For example, if you are afraid of quitting your job, start imagining what your new job would be like. What kind of new job would you like to have? Imagine yourself in this new place and how you would feel. If you wish to be self-employed, take a day off and pretend you already are. How would you spend your day? The joy you will feel imagining or pretending to be in your new life will replace your fear. This joy will attract to you what you really want and give you the courage to move forward. Our outer life is always a reflection of our inner life. When we are fearful, we attract what we fear. When we are joyful, we attract more of what makes us happy.

When you notice you are in fear, ask yourself if your fear is really justified, make an action plan to eliminate each one of your fears, and move forward with courage and confidence in the direction of your dreams. Imagine your dream life. Use your imagination to bring yourself into a state of joy, fulfillment, grace, and love. It is these emotions that will attract to you the amazing life of your dreams!

It's like the saying "Feel the fear and do it anyway!" That is what I have been doing these last three years since I left my job and my family and friends and sold my house, my furniture, and my car, all to pursue this calling I have in my heart the desire to share with you my love for the angels. I have been learning to move past my fears and stay centered in faith. I trust that I am being guided and cared for each and every step of the way. And I can attest to you that everything I have needed so far has been provided. I live a much simpler life but certainly a happier and more fulfilling one.

Have I been afraid? Of course. There are days when I feel overwhelmed by fear, but I go outside for a walk or meditate and I pray to the angels.

When I feel in fear, I stop and ask myself, "What am I so afraid of?" Once I know exactly what I fear, I pray to the angels to help with that. My prayers are always a prayer of gratitude in advance for that which I need or desire: "Thank you, thank you, thank you, my darling angels, for taking care of me and all my needs. Thank you for the courage and strength to keep moving forward fearlessly. Thank you for _____."

Next, I make an action plan and get busy. Fear often creeps in when we are not busy enough. When we are focused on the task at hand, we have no time to be afraid.

The Power of Prayer

Prayer is one of the most powerful methods we can use to transform our lives and overcome fear. When we pray with conviction, believing that someone or something greater than ourselves is working on our behalf, miracles can happen.

Many people today are living with much anxiety, stress, and fear and do not realize the power of prayer. Just the other day, a friend of mine who has been battling anxiety for the past ten years finally realized that in her parents and grandparents' day, they handled their stress and anxiety with prayer. "Most people don't think about praying," she said. Like her, they struggle through life alone or in therapy and with drugs. Know that the angels are here to help you, and remember that they cannot help you unless you ask.

I, myself, was going through a difficult period recently. After being married for only eighteen short months, I was very unhappy and realized I had made a mistake. I was filled with shame, guilt, and fear. I knew deep down in my heart that this was not the life God and the angels wanted for me. My inspiration was gone, as well as my joy for living. I had no self-esteem, no self-confidence, no energy, and no desire to continue living my life as it was. At the same time, I felt paralyzed by fear. I was stuck and didn't know how I was going to get myself out of it. I had become financially dependent and was in debt. I felt trapped. I started to wonder how I was going to find the strength and courage to right the wrong. I was afraid to tell my husband, my family, my friends, and my clients. I was afraid to disappoint all the people I loved.

Many of you will ask, "Well, didn't you receive any signs before you got married?" Yes, I did. I knew in my gut that something was off, but I just couldn't make sense of it. He had everything I had wanted in a person, but I had this feeling I could not shake. I know people say, "If you have doubts, don't." Well, that is true, but sometimes it's easier said than done. Sometimes we don't have the strength to do the right thing, so we go along until one day we find it. And when we finally feel strong enough to do the right thing, the angels say to be proud of ourselves for finally doing what we know is true in our heart and not beat ourselves up because we didn't do it sooner. Better late than never.

Every experience brings a lesson. I've learned that I really need to trust and listen to my gut feeling, whether I understand it or not. I have learned to love and respect myself more and to be more assertive. I have a new sense of strength and self-worth that I did not have before that relationship. Every experience holds a blessing, and I am grateful for my newfound strength and confidence.

This is the type of situation in which fear will lead us. I was so afraid of hurting him and the people around me that I ended up hurting myself the most.

Prayer is what saved me. It gave me the strength and the courage to do the right thing.

A friend of mine had spoken to me about the Prayer of Saint Francis, and upon reading it, I felt this strong desire well up inside of me and thought, "That's what I want my life to be about." So one morning, I shared the Prayer of Saint Francis on my Facebook page:

> *Lord, make me an instrument of your peace.*
> *Where there is hatred, let me sow love;*
> *Where there is injury, pardon;*
> *Where there is doubt, faith;*
> *Where there is despair, hope;*
> *Where there is darkness, light;*
> *Where there is sadness, joy.*
>
> *O Divine Master, grant that I may not so much seek*
> *To be consoled as to console,*
> *To be understood as to understand,*
> *To be loved as to love;*

For it is in giving that we receive;
It is in pardoning that we are pardoned;
And it is in dying that we are born to eternal life.

The next day, I felt inspired to write and share my own prayer. I sensed that others might be experiencing their own difficulties and maybe my prayer could help. So my first prayer looked like this:

Dear God and my loving angels, you know I have been experiencing difficulties lately. Thank you for helping me not only get through this difficult period but transform it. Thank you for your mercy and your blessings. Thank you, God and my dearest angels, for renewing my faith both in you and myself.

I composed and shared a prayer every day afterward. Twelve days after sharing that first prayer, I felt the courage to leave my marriage. It took every ounce of strength I had, but I knew that my soul would die if I stayed. And I knew that if I stayed, he would look at me one day and say, "You are not the person I married," and of course I wouldn't have been, because she was dying a little every day. I knew that I would have woken up ten years down the road totally disconnected from my true self and alone.

Seventy-five days after posting that first Prayer of Saint Francis, the angels whispered to me that my prayer had been answered. They said, "Go read it and see!" I went back to my first post on January 30th and cried as they told me that by sharing my own daily prayers, I had sown love, pardon, faith, hope, light, and joy in the lives of others. I had consoled, understood, and loved them. By giving, I had received. I forgave and was forgiven.

And most importantly, the old me had died and I was reborn. My life had completely transformed in those seventy-five days. I had left my husband, moved back to Quebec City, and taken my life back. Was it all easy? No. I did some crying and a lot of praying. I reached out to friends who were there for me and loved me through the experience without judgment. It was heart-warming to hear a friend say, "You are the strongest person I know," or having my family stand by my decision and say, "The only thing that matters is that you're happy. We love you no matter what."

I know that not everyone will understand your decision to love and honor what you know to be true in your heart. We all make so-called mistakes in our lives; we take detours and gain experiences. Know that you are always headed in the right direction. We live and learn. Every experience brings us a lesson and a gentle message that says, "Love yourself more." Let go of all your fears, including the ones about what other people might think, and move forward fearlessly. Be true to yourself and your calling. Learn to obey the guidance of your angels immediately without question.

Know that you are never alone. God and the angels love you and will never judge you or leave you. They only want you to be happy. They wait patiently by your side, waiting for you to call upon them. Pray to them and know that your prayers will always be answered. You just have to believe.

If you are feeling the desire to change your own life right now, ask the angels to help you let go of the fear. Here are a couple of prayers that may help you tame your fears and move forward with strength and courage. They have helped me.

Dear God and my loving angels, thank you for helping me tame my fears. I know that fear is just a sign of my lack of faith in you and your goodness. Please help me remember that all things are possible through you. Like any loving parent, you love me and care for me and you will never let me down. Please help me trust in your divine plan for my life and know that all is well. I trust that I am safe.

Thank you, God and my darling angels, for guiding me forward, for helping me look past my fears to see only opportunities and love in the future, and for giving me the strength and courage to follow your guidance. Thank you, thank you, thank you.

I have found prayer and meditation to be the most effective ways to conquer my own fears of moving forward and of the unknown. I pray to the angels to help build my faith in them and in their divine plan.

To help you build your own faith, the angels suggest you look back at your life and see how they have always been there for you and how everything has always worked out. When you can see that God and your loving angels have always been there by your side, you can more easily move forward, one step at time and with confidence, trusting that all is well and that you are never alone.

Prayer to Release Fear

To help you release fears of moving forward, I offer you the following prayer.

Worthiness

"Lord God, I am worthy of your goodness, your grace, and your blessings. With your help, I am willing to release all fears that are preventing me from moving forward. I know that my will is your will and you only want what is best for me."

Desire

"Dearest angels, I deeply desire _____."

Trust

"My dearest angels, I trust you completely. I know that you are with me every step of the way. I promise you, Lord God and my dearest angels, to always look at my fears and take action to diminish them and to listen to your divine guidance. I will stay open to and follow all the signs you will send my way."

Imagination

I reserve at least ten minutes a day to imagine that I am already realizing my dreams. I imagine the joy, the love, and the wholeness I feel in this new life that I live fearlessly.

Gratitude

"Thank you in advance, Lord God and my dearest angels, for helping me with my confidence in you, in myself, and in life. Thank you for the courage, strength, and determination to move forward fearlessly. I am grateful for your presence, your assistance, and your guidance. Thank you, thank you, thank you."

EXERCISE
Fear

Too often we let our fears take over and keep us prisoners of our lives. Get in the habit of looking at what is preventing you from moving forward and creating the life you want.

Look at your life to see where fear may be stopping you and cutting off your momentum. See what solutions you might find to overcome your fears and finally live the life of your dreams. Remember that you are never alone.

Worthiness

Write down your fears, the worst things you think could happen to you. For example:

+ "I'm afraid of not succeeding."
+ "I'm afraid of running out of money."

For each of your fears, ask yourself if it is really justified. Then release all your fears:

+ "I release the fear of not succeeding."
+ "I release the fear of running out of money."

Now create new beliefs:

+ "I succeed in all I do."
+ "Everything I need is being provided to me."

Desire

Describe your dreams.

Trust

Look at each one of your fears and see what actions could be taken to overcome or diminish them. Ask your angels to help you find solutions to diminish your fears and to propose actions to help increase your confidence. Stay open to divine guidance.

For each one of your fears, find an action to diminish it. Her are some examples:

Fear	Actions
Fear of failure	Doing my best each and every day
Fear of being short of money	Save money; establish a budget and follow it

Imagination

Describe in great detail how you would live your life fearlessly.

Gratitude

Write down what makes you grateful.

- "I am grateful for the courage, strength and determination to move forward."
- "I am grateful for your presence, your assistance and your guidance."

15

Love

"Love and life are the same.
When there is no love, there is no life."
—*Roch Carrier*

You are destined to have a wonderful life! You are meant to be happy, to be healthy, to be in love, to have abundance, and to live the life of your dreams. You are destined to fulfill your life's purpose, to feel good about yourself, to have relationships that make you happy, and to have enough money to pay your bills. And all of this is possible with love, for love heals everything. Make sure there is love in all areas of your life and see your life transform!

The angels suggest we do everything with love, no matter how menial the task may be. If you are cleaning your home, do it with love. If you are working at a job that may not be exactly what you want to be doing right now, do it with love. The angels suggest we *love it to death*; love it so it can die and be transformed into something more wonderful and aligned with what you really want.

We all live through times in our lives when we are in a place or a situation where we are unhappy. If this is where you find yourself right now, ask the angels to help you love it to death: "My darling angels, thank you for helping me do what I must do for now, with love. I know that this too shall pass. Help me see the blessings in this situation or task at hand. I know that the more love I sincerely give to it, the quicker it will transform. Thank you, thank you, thank you."

When I lived in Ontario, I was unhappy. I felt alone and far away from my family and friends. I knew in my heart that the angels wanted me to be at peace. I knew I had to learn to *love the place to death* if I had any hope of moving on. So I prayed to the angels to help me find peace, joy, and love in my situation. That is when I met my neighbor who introduced me to Reiki, made new friends, and discovered new things that I loved. I was guided to move on when I finally felt at peace with the place.

The angels also suggest that you send love to any situation that you have difficulty with, such as when someone has done you wrong. I know this can be disheartening, but the angels suggest you send the person love. Allow yourself to feel angry and disappointed for a day or two, but quickly come back to that space inside of yourself where love resides and then send them love. The more love you send, the quicker you will heal and move forward. Say, "Thank you, my darling angels, for helping me send love to _____. I sincerely wish them love and all the best. I know greater love exists for me, and the more I stay in a state of love and grace, the more love I will receive."

The angels also invite us to always do things *out of* love and not *for* love. When we do things *for* love, we are actually doing them out of fear. We are doing things with the expectation of receiving love in return. Therefore, we are not being loving toward ourselves, nor are we being loving toward others. We are really afraid of not being good enough, of not being loved. So only do things from the goodness of your heart.

There are only two basic emotions in life: fear and love. If you are in fear, you cannot be in love.

Where do these emotions come from? They come from your thoughts. And the good news is you have control over your thoughts.

The angels recommend that you keep your thoughts positive to create positive things in your life. If you focus on what you love, that is what you will attract. So let loose and love more! Look at what you love in your life and speak it out loud.

I say, "I love my life! I love myself! I love my family, my environment, and my friends. I love my body, my face, my hair, my teeth! I love my new home! I love my car! I love the sun, the beach, and the blue sky. I love beautiful things. I love to pay my bills. I love being able to pay for all my basic needs and little luxuries. I love traveling and meeting new people. I love to write. I love doing readings for my clients and making them happy. I love to share. I love that God and the angels support me in all my efforts to live my passion. I love that the angels always guide me to the right person, at the right place and at the right time. I love that I am guided to take the right actions to achieve my dreams. I love that they bless me with grace every day! I love that I am creating an amazing life beyond my wildest dreams!"

Make a list of everything you love. List the things you already have and what you want to attract into your life, and remember what is most important is to *feel the love.*

Thoughts create, but emotions create even faster, so *feel* the love.

When you send something out into the universe, it comes back to you tenfold. If you send love, you will receive love in abundance.

When you send fear into the universe, it also comes back to you tenfold, so it is better to invest your energy in what is best for you!

Love attracts love, so when you see something you love, say so! When you show God and the angels what you love, you attract it to you. The reverse is also true. When you show God and the angels what you do not like, you also attract that to you.

For example, in 2011 I left the office with a colleague for a coffee break and I saw a beautiful convertible go by. I said to my colleague, "Wow! Did you see that beautiful car? It is my dream to have a convertible one day, but I would like one with a hard top!" I did not even know such a car existed. The next morning, I took my little eight-year-old Volkswagen Golf to the garage for regular maintenance, and while I waited for them to take me back to the office, I noticed a brochure with a picture of a white convertible with a hardtop—the Volkswagen Eos. My heart skipped a beat. I took the brochure, and when the manager drove me to my office, I asked him about the car. He said they just happened to have one sitting in the parking lot if I wanted to try it out when I returned to pick up my car at the end of the day.

After work, the manager was waiting for me outside with the key. He had a dark blue Eos parked out front with the top down. He handed me the key and told me to bring it back after dinner. So I picked up my mother, my niece, and her friend and we drove around town several times. What an experience! People often say that to try it is to adopt it. This was certainly the case. Since I had recently sold my house, I decided I could afford to buy myself a little luxury. I told myself it was no different than a man buying himself a big truck. Why not spoil myself a little? I had the money, and life showed me that my dream car existed. I ordered a candy-white Eos—a color that represents purity, summer, and fun at the beach. It suited me perfectly!

When we admire something that someone else has, we attract it to us, but when we envy what another has, we send negative energy into the universe and we push away what we really desire for ourselves. It is so important to be happy for other people, because that positive emotion will attract to us the desired object or situation. Be happy for your friend who received a promotion, for your neighbor who bought a new home, or for your sister who is taking her dream vacation. Feel only love for everything good that is happening in the lives of others. When you are happy for the success of another person, it is like saying to the universe, "I would like that too!"

The angels also suggest that we be loving toward everyone we meet. Resist the temptation to judge others. Judging is not being loving.

Let me share an example of how judgment can attract a so-called negative situation. I went out with a guy for two and a half years. After the first six months, he said to me one day, "I don't think I'm in love with you!" Despite his admission, we remained together for two more years. When I finally left, I questioned with very strong emotion, "How could he stay with me all this time without being in love?" I could not understand but really wanted to.

A few years later, I dated another guy for fourteen months. And when I left him, it popped into my mind that I had spent all that time with him without being in love. The relationship was convenient at the time for various reasons. Life had brought me the exact same situation in reverse to help me understand. This is when I realized that we should never judge or condemn others, because we will attract to us the very same situation to help us understand what others are living.

At the same time that I was being taught this lesson, an acquaintance of mine experienced a similar situation. She had judged her best friend severely when her husband had left her friend for another woman, so much so that she had severed ties with her friend. Remember, we attract what we judge and need to understand. Shortly thereafter, this woman's husband also left her for another woman.

When you ask, "But how could that person have done such a thing?" it is like saying to the universe, "I want to understand how that person could do such a thing!" Be very careful. Do not judge or condemn, because life will help you understand.

Try to see love in every situation in your life and be loving and understanding toward others. If you are experiencing a difficult situation, ask the angels to help you transform it with love. Love is always the answer. Always ask, "What would love do?" The answer will come to you.

When you look at life through the eyes of love, you see beyond appearances. You see the perfection of everything that exists around you. You see that the person who irritated you or hurt you also has fears. You develop compassion for others. With love, you can understand what is not obvious at first glance: the fact that each person is a divine being, a child of God. Every person is living their own fears. When you look with the eyes of your heart at a person who intimidated you or wronged you, you will understand that this person is simply afraid of losing your love.

Remember that each person does their best with the knowledge they have. You may be disappointed with a person you love, like your mother, your father, your spouse, your friend, but know that this person is doing their best with the knowledge they have. When we know better, we do better. Do not hesitate to ask your angels to help you find love and compassion for those around you. Focus your attention on what is positive in the person; maybe they have a big heart for children and animals, or maybe they are involved in a charity. Everyone has something good inside of them. Ask your angels to help you discover it if you have difficulty.

Know that you also need love. You need your own love. Love yourself. Be kind and gentle with yourself and never demean yourself, thinking that you are less than others. You are perfect just as you are. The angels say we are much too hard on ourselves.

When you think, "My God, I'm fat!" you are attracting even more weight to yourself. Similarly, if you say, "My God, I am wrinkled!" it will attract even more wrinkles. The angels suggest you go buy yourself clothes that will make you feel beautiful. They exist. When I put on weight, I go buy myself new pants a size larger so I feel thinner, and after a few weeks I lose the extra pounds. Wearing bigger pants makes me feel beautiful and slim, and that is what I attract.

There is a solution to every problem, and more love is always the solution. Ask, "How can I love myself more?" For wrinkles, I apply cream every day and night. I pay close attention to how I apply it as well. When I apply my face cream, I caress my face and tell my skin how beautiful it is. The fact that I take care of my face shows it the love I have for it. If you do not like something about yourself, give even more love to this part of your body. Pour the lotion on your thighs, your belly, your breasts, etc., and tell them, "I love you!"

Look at your body and your face with love and compassion. Look at yourself in the mirror and tell yourself every morning and evening, "I love you! Although _____, I love you anyway!" Be your own best friend.

When you hear bad news, either on TV or in your life, send love to the situation. Say, "Dear angels, thank you for helping me send love, peace, and understanding to the people who are living a difficult time. Help them understand and accept what they are living. Help them understand that this event is part of a larger plan of which only God and the souls involved know the purpose."

When your friend confides in you about what she is experiencing, try to listen with your heart. Be understanding. If you have trouble with this, ask your angels to help you open your heart. If you judge, you will attract to you the same situation to help you better understand it. The angels gave me the idea that we can imagine seeing others through heart-shaped glasses to see others with love. Another idea is to imagine yourself inside a huge heart in 3-D. This heart will be between you and others to remind you to remain in your heart. Awesome!

Be love in all your interactions: with yourself, your family, your friends, your neighbors, your community, and your planet.

Be gentle and compassionate with yourself and your loved ones. Forgive yourself and others. Thank God and the angels for everyone who is a part of your life. Send them love and gratitude. Take care of your community. Help your neighbors. A well-intentioned prayer can create miracles. Do your part for the planet. Be a conscious consumer. Reduce your carbon footprint. Be love.

Love is the greatest force in the universe. In fact, the universe is love. God is love. We are love. Love heals everything. So we can conclude that we are also God, we are love, and we can heal everything.

EXERCISE
Love

Love attracts love. Make a list of everything you love in life. List all the things you already have and also what you want to attract in the future. Remember that the most important thing is to *feel the love.*

Thoughts create, but emotions create even faster, so *feel* the love. For example:

- "I love my life!"
- "I love _____."

When we admire something that someone else has, we attract it to us, but when we envy what another has, we send negative energy into the universe and push away what we really desire for ourselves. It is so important to be happy for other people.

What do you admire about others? Write it down. Here are some examples:

- "I admire people who follow their passion."
- "I admire people who travel the world sharing their passion with others."

Then rewrite the sentences:

- "I, too, desire to follow my passion!"
- "I, too, desire to travel the world sharing my passion with others."

Prayer for Love

"Lord God and my beloved angels, help me to see myself with love and compassion, help me to see others with the same love and compassion, and help me to feel love for my enemies, my attackers, and all those who have done me wrong. With your support, I send them love and pray for their well-being.

"Lord God and my beloved angels, help me to send love, peace, and understanding to those who are experiencing difficult times. Help them understand and accept the situation with grace. Help me see the perfection in my own life and in every situation that presents itself to me. Thank you, Lord God and my darling angels, for your unconditional love. It is my greatest desire to love myself and others as purely as you do.

"Thank you, thank you, thank you!"

16
FAITH

"I can see how it might be possible for a man to look down upon the earth and be an atheist, but I cannot conceive how he could look up into the heavens and say there is no God."
—*Abraham Lincoln*

We often hear people say, "I'll believe it when I see it!" But, in fact, you have to believe to see! Unfortunately, these people must not notice the miracles that surround them. We are surrounded by miracles every day. You just have to observe the beauty of nature to see it. It starts with the sunrise—what a miracle in and of itself! Then notice the snow melting day after day in the spring, leaving nature to wake up after a long winter. What a miracle it is to see the new grass having the courage to poke through the dead grass underneath! Life begins again. Nature renews itself every year as if by magic. The birds sing their songs that seem to tell other animals to wake up, because spring is in the air. Nature continues its cycle until summer, when the flowers are opening and deciduous trees are in full bloom! It is all so miraculous!

Every evening, the sun sets and the moon rises in turn. The stars shine and watch over us, comforting us and cooling us after a hot summer day.

This cycle allows the earth to produce food for animals, nests for their young, and heat for their survival. In the fall, the animals prepare for the winter months, a time when everything will rest and recharge before coming alive again in the spring. But notice that trees grow several inches every year, and every spring they do not start at zero but continue their evolution from year to year, just like us.

The cycle of days and seasons is proof that there is something bigger than us out there that ensures our survival.

Do you not see that same magic in your own life? Have you not noticed how magically things always seem to work out? That just like the birds, you were never really missing anything? That you have always met the right person at the right time? And how things have always fallen into place for you, as if by chance?

Just as God and the angels care for the animals and the plants, they care for you and your survival. They have always been there beside you. God has sent angels to protect you and guide you toward a better life that is in line with the deepest desires of your heart, and this without you even asking.

Imagine what they could do if you asked!

Often, when I make a special request, I end it with the following phrase: "I know, God and my darling angels, that you care for the birds and I know you also care for me." I have complete faith. I believe that God and the angels are there for me. I know they want me to be happy and to fulfill my life's purpose. So I know that if I ask them for something that will help me fulfill my purpose, that will help me better serve others, this request will be granted.

God has planted a seed of passion in each one of our hearts. He has given us all the gifts we need, provided us with all the right tools, and even sent us loving divine helpers we call angels to help us achieve our dreams. Be confident that if you have a dream that is dear to your heart and you do your part to achieve it, God and the angels will do everything they can to help make your dream come true. This is where we must have faith. Just as we can be certain that the caterpillar will turn into a butterfly one day, you too will be transformed into a state of unimaginable beauty and grace.

Dare to dream! Dare to ask! Dare to believe!

EXERCISE
Faith

We often hear people say, "I'll believe it when I see it! " But when it comes to faith, you have to believe to see!

Take a look at your life and see all the times when you were loved and supported through a difficult period. Make a list of all the times you have been afraid of not having enough, afraid to change, to move, to love, or to take a risk, and remember how things have always worked out for you, how you've always been cared for, and how you've always succeeded no matter what.

When you pray to God and the angels for something specific, end it with this phrase: "I know, God and my loving angels, that you care for the birds and I know you also care for me."

17

GRATITUDE

"One single grateful thought raised to heaven
is the most perfect prayer."
—*G. E. Lessing*

One January morning, I went downstairs in our new house and noticed that our Christmas tree had already been taken down and put outside. I felt upset because I had really wanted to take the time to thank the tree for having spent the holidays with us. This may seem strange to you, but I believe it is important to express gratitude for all that is in our life, even the so-called inanimate objects.

My boyfriend and I had found this tree at a discount at the end of the day on Christmas Eve. The saleswoman explained that they had received the wrong order and that the trees were not the beautiful farmed Christmas trees they had ordered. I didn't care. I just really wanted to have a Christmas tree.

We had just moved into our new house. The cupboards had no doors and there were boxes scattered everywhere, but it was Christmas and I wanted to celebrate it.

This poor tree looked like a Charlie Brown Christmas tree. Digging through my boxes, I found ten red balls, two sets of beads, and a string of lights. Despite the tree having only a few decorations, I was still pleased to have a tree and I appreciated it.

The morning I found the tree lying outside on the patio, I thought to myself, "I should get dressed and go outside to thank it." But something told me that it was not necessary, that the tree would hear me from inside the house. So I stood by the window and talked to the tree. I told it how grateful and happy I was to have had the opportunity to share this Christmas with it. I was happy that it was able to fulfill its life's purpose to celebrate Christmas. There were still hundreds of trees at the stores that were not so lucky. Talking to the tree, I felt that it was talking back to me. It communicated to me that its life would not end there, but in fact it was going to be transformed once it was recycled with the other trees. I was relieved to know that it had accepted its fate. The tree seemed to know why it was there, and it was okay with that. Everything was perfect in its world. I started to send the tree lots of love and gratitude when suddenly I felt a wave of love come rushing back to me.

I felt amazed and shaken at the same time. It was as if a hose connected us to each other and the love was flowing back and forth between us. All the love I felt for the tree came rushing back to me multiplied. I felt tears well up in my eyes and felt my heart expand.

And then, I felt the love of all the things around me: the balcony, the entrance, the cars, the lampposts, the houses, the sky, and all the space in between these things. Love was coming from everywhere. I started to cry, because the emotion was so strong that I could not contain it. I felt that everything was love and I, too, was part of this love. Everything started to sparkle. It was as if a veil of lively sparkles covered reality. It was as if I was seeing through another dimension that is not usually perceivable. I felt such an amazing sense of peace, serenity, and love that I did not want the experience to end. But after a few seconds, everything went back to normal. It was such an extraordinary experience! I know there are people who meditate all their lives wishing to have such an experience. I feel so blessed to have experienced such all-encompassing love in a moment of simple but immense gratitude.

This experience of gratitude helped me understand just how much the universe, God, and the angels love us. In fact, it taught me that we are love and that all that exists is love. Love is the only thing that is real and the rest is an illusion.

"Gr-attitude" is an attitude of grace; it is a state of mind where one recognizes God's favor and blessings.

Gratitude is a conversation, a prayer of thanks to the divine. It is how we recognize the presence of the divine in our lives.

"Thank you" is the single most important prayer you will ever need. With these two simple words, you are telling God and the angels that you are aware that you are not alone, you are grateful for all the goodness you already have in your life, and you trust that you are being cared for.

With those two simple words, you can create a magnificent life even greater than you could ever imagine, because saying thank you is like saying to God and the angels, "I believe in you. I believe in your goodness, your grace, and your blessings."

When you send something out into the universe, it comes back to you multiplied. If you send love, you will receive love multiplied. If you send gratitude, the universe will thank you too. It will send you more blessings and grace for which to be grateful.

The angels recommend you write down every day in your journal at least three things you are grateful for today and three things you would like to attract in the future (but write them in the present tense).

While working on this book, I was doing some house cleaning and found a gratitude journal that my sister had given me. I opened it up to a page, and this is what I had written that I wanted to attract:

February 3, 2009

I am so grateful to have found a publishing house for my book!
I am so grateful that my book is published in French!
And I am so grateful that my book is such a big success!

The fact of having come across this journal entry at the end of writing this book in French was a sign from the angels confirming that when we are grateful in advance for something that we strongly desire, they have already begun to fulfill it. Know that we must do our part. I had finally decided to write a book in French, and I followed the guidance that led me to the publishing house. This left me to believe that my third wish, that my book would be successful, would come true. And it did! It became a national bestseller in only four months in the province of Quebec alone.

Today, I am also very grateful! I am grateful to the angels for guiding me to my English publisher, Llewellyn Worldwide. I am grateful to all my clients and friends who have inspired and encouraged me to write and translate this book. I hope it lives up to your expectations!

I am grateful to God and the archangels and angels for their inspiration, divine guidance, and presence in my life. I am also grateful for all the wonderful opportunities to share with the world their teachings, their guidance, and their love.

I am grateful to you, dear reader, for your time and for reading this book. Thank you for having given yourself this time to read and reflect, to believe in yourself and in your dreams, and to build your faith in God and the angels. It is my greatest desire that you find your life's purpose, your inner light, so that you too may light the way for others.

May your life be filled with meaning, health, money, and abundance, and may it overflow with energy, joy, and love!

May God and the angels bless you and may their grace always be with you!

Thank you, thank you, thank you!

EXERCISE
Gratitude

Present

Saying thank you is the greatest gift you can give to God and the angels.

Each day, write down three things you are grateful for. For example:

- "Thank you, God and my loving angels, for the inspiration and guidance to write this book."

- "Thank you, God and my loving angels, for _____."

Future Desires

Write down future events for which you are grateful. Write them in the present tense. Being grateful in advance is like saying, "And so it is!"

- "I am so grateful for all the wonderful opportunities to share God's grace and the angels' loving messages with so many people around the world!"

- "I am so grateful for _____!"

APPENDIX
List of Other Archangels

Ariel

This archangel is known for his desire to care for the environment. If you feel your life's purpose has to do with protecting the environment, the oceans, or animals, call on Archangel Ariel to help you with your mission.

Azrael

Archangel Azrael is present to those who are dying and their families. He helps the dying with their transition and aids their family in the grieving process. If you are grieving the loss of a loved one or if your life's purpose involves grief counseling, assisting the dying, or working as a medium, call on Archangel Azrael to help you with your grieving process or your mission.

Chamuel

Archangel Chamuel is known to be one of the power archangels and is very protective of the earth and its inhabitants. He will help you let go of any fears you have about your future or the future of the planet. You can call on him to protect you from lower energies of living people or earthbound spirits. If you work as a medium, Archangel Chamuel can protect you.

Haniel

Archangel Haniel helps with many different things, such as clairvoyance and receiving guidance about healing, self-esteem, self-confidence, and self-assurance. You can call on Archangel Haniel to receive guidance about healing yourself or others and to help you with your self-confidence before an event or about making big decisions in your life.

Jeremiel

Archangel Jeremiel is known to help with topics related to our third eye, such as our life review and clairvoyance. He helps newly crossed-over souls do their life review, and he can also help us here on earth to review our life now to better realign our intentions for the future. You can also call on him to help you open your third eye.

Jophiel

Archangel Jophiel is feminine energy who can help you with beautifying your life and your environment. She can help you declutter your environment, embellish your home, and see beauty in everything around you. She also encourages you to work on artistic projects to better connect with the divine.

Metatron

Archangel Metatron is a very large archangel who holds all the knowledge of our akashic records and higher wisdom. He assists therapists who help people heal their past lives as well as their past in this lifetime. He also works very closely with highly sensitive children, and you can call upon him to help find natural solutions to assist your sensitive child or to help them adapt in this world.

Raguel

Archangel Raguel is known to bring harmony to your relationships. He can help heal any relationship by bringing mediation, resolution, and peace. He is particularly good at helping you resolve conflict. Call upon him when you need to find a positive and peaceful resolution to a conflict. He is an excellent counselor, mediator, and motivator. If your profession involves any of these domains, call on him to help you be your best.

Raziel

Archangel Raziel helps us use our accumulated knowledge and experience from all of our past lives and focus them into our present life's mission. He helps us to stay focused and motivated and to resist temptations that distract us from our purpose. He can help with the development of our extrasensory perceptions and gifts. Call upon Archangel Raziel for higher wisdom on any subject and allow him to guide you through your clear senses. He is also great at helping you manifest your desires.

Sandalphon

Archangel Sandalphon's principal role is to bring your prayers to heaven. He is also the patron of musicians. Call upon Archangel Sandalphon when you have an urgent prayer you need answered or if you are a struggling musician or are learning to play a new instrument.

Zadkiel

Archangel Zadkiel is the archangel of compassion and forgiveness. He helps us see others with love and understanding so we may more easily forgive. He also helps with our memory and to find lost objects.

To Write to the Author

If you wish to contact the author or would like more information about this book, please write to the author in care of Llewellyn Worldwide and we will forward your request. Both the author and the publisher appreciate hearing from you and learning of your enjoyment of this book and how it has helped you. Llewellyn Worldwide cannot guarantee that every letter written to the author can be answered, but all will be forwarded. Please write to:

Lucinda Gabriel
℅ Llewellyn Worldwide
2143 Wooddale Drive
Woodbury, MN 55125.2989

Please enclose a self-addressed stamped envelope for reply, or $1.00 to cover costs. If outside the U.S.A., enclose an international postal reply coupon.

You can also contact the author directly through her website:
www.lucindagabriel.com